O9-ABE-969

The Great Depression

Other Books in the Turning Points Series:

The Great Depression

Don Nardo, *Book Editor*

David L. Bender, *Publisher*
Bruno Leone, *Executive Editor*
Bonnie Szumski, *Editorial Director*
David M. Haugen, *Managing Editor*

Delafield Public Library
Delafield, WI 53018

Greenhaven Press, Inc., San Diego, California

Every effort has been made to trace the owners of copyrighted material. The articles in this volume may have been edited for content, length, and/or reading level. The titles have been changed to enhance the editorial purpose.

No part of this book may be reproduced or used in any form or by any means, electrical, mechanical, or otherwise, including, but not limited to, photocopy, recording, or any information storage and retrieval system, without prior written permission from the publisher.

Library of Congress Cataloging-in-Publication Data
The Great Depression / Don Nardo, book editor.
    p.   cm. — (Turning points in world history)
    Includes bibliographical references and index.
    ISBN 0-7377-0230-3 (pbk. : alk. paper). —
ISBN 0-7377-0231-1 (lib. bdg. : alk. paper)
    1. Depressions—1929—United States. 2. United States—
Economic conditions—1918–1945. 3. United States—Economic
policy—1933–1945. 4. New Deal, 1933–1939. I. Nardo, Don,
1947– . II. Series: Turning points in world history (Greenhaven
Press)
HB3717 1929.G686 2000
338.5'42—dc21   99-28801
                                                                 CIP

Cover photo: Library of Congress

©2000 by Greenhaven Press, Inc.
P.O. Box 289009, San Diego, CA 92198-9009

Printed in the U.S.A.

3 0646 00133 4261

Contents

of major reform bills, an auspicious beginning for the ambitious New Deal that promised to put the country on its feet.

Chapter 4: New Deal Programs, Policies, and Controversies

Foreword

Certain past events stand out as pivotal, as having effects and outcomes that change the course of history. These events are often referred to as turning points. Historian Louis L. Snyder provides this useful definition:

A turning point in history is an event, happening, or stage which thrusts the course of historical development into a different direction. By definition a turning point is a great event, but it is even more—a great event with the explosive impact of altering the trend of man's life on the planet.

History's turning points have taken many forms. Some were single, brief, and shattering events with immediate and obvious impact. The invasion of Britain by William the Conqueror in 1066, for example, swiftly transformed that land's political and social institutions and paved the way for the rise of the modern English nation. By contrast, other single events were deemed of minor significance when they occurred, only later recognized as turning points. The assassination of a little-known European nobleman, Archduke Franz Ferdinand, on June 28, 1914, in the Bosnian town of Sarajevo was such an event; only after it touched off a chain reaction of political-military crises that escalated into the global conflict known as World War I did the murder's true significance become evident.

Other crucial turning points occurred not in terms of a few hours, days, months, or even years, but instead as evolutionary developments spanning decades or even centuries. One of the most pivotal turning points in human history, for instance—the development of agriculture, which replaced nomadic hunter-gatherer societies with more permanent settlements—occurred over the course of many generations. Still other great turning points were neither events nor developments, but rather revolutionary new inventions and innovations that significantly altered social customs and ideas, military tactics, home life, the spread of knowledge, and the human condition in general. The developments of writing, gunpowder, the printing press, antibiotics, the electric light, atomic energy, television, and the computer, the last two of which have recently ushered in the world-altering information age, represent only some of these innovative turning points.

Each anthology in the Greenhaven Turning Points in World History series presents a group of essays chosen for their accessibility. The anthology's structure also enhances this accessibility. First, an introductory essay provides a general overview of the principal events and figures involved, placing the topic in its historical context. The essays that follow explore various aspects in more detail, some targeting political trends and consequences, others social, literary, cultural, and/or technological ramifications, and still others pivotal leaders and other influential figures. To aid the reader in choosing the material of immediate interest or need, each essay is introduced by a concise summary of the contributing writer's main themes and insights.

In addition, each volume contains extensive research tools, including a collection of excerpts from primary source documents pertaining to the historical events and figures under discussion. In the anthology on the French Revolution, for example, readers can examine the works of Rousseau, Voltaire, and other writers and thinkers whose championing of human rights helped fuel the French people's growing desire for liberty; the French *Declaration of the Rights of Man and Citizen*, presented to King Louis XVI by the French National Assembly on October 2, 1789; and eyewitness accounts of the attack on the royal palace and the horrors of the Reign of Terror. To guide students interested in pursuing further research on the subject, each volume features an extensive bibliography, which for easy access has been divided into separate sections by topic. Finally, a comprehensive index allows readers to scan and locate content efficiently. Each of the anthologies in the Greenhaven Turning Points in World History series provides students with a complete, detailed, and enlightening examination of a crucial historical watershed.

Introduction: The Great Depression and the New Deal

During the last ten days of October 1929, the New York Stock Exchange suffered a series of largely unexpected and devastating blows. In the afternoon of October 21, stocks suddenly slumped sharply in the heaviest trading on record; trading was so intense, in fact, that by the end of the day the ticker machine used to record transactions was running a hundred minutes behind the actual sales. The situation got only worse in the days that followed. On Monday, October 28, for instance, the market registered an unprecedented loss of $14 billion. And the next day it took another enormous jolt, losing $15 billion and bringing the losses for the month to a staggering $50 billion. Historian Gerald W. Johnson explains how the effects of this disaster quickly rippled outward, engulfing the rest of society:

> When the panic of 1929 suddenly wiped out the whole value of many stocks and sharply reduced the values of others, a great number of people who had thought themselves rich, or at least well-off, found themselves with much less than they had thought they had, or with nothing at all. By [the] millions they quit buying anything except what they had to have to stay alive. This drop in spending threw the stores into trouble, and they quit ordering [new products] and discharged clerks. When orders stopped the factories shut down, and factory workers had no jobs.[1]

Thanks to this destructive financial chain reaction, the great stock market crash unleashed the onslaught of a severe economic depression that affected not only the United States, but most of the rest of the industrialized world as well.[2] It became known as the "Great Depression" because it was the worst financial crisis ever recorded in modern times. For up to a decade or more, tens of millions of Americans and hundreds of millions of people worldwide fell into grinding, seemingly unrelenting poverty and suffered untold deprivations and miseries.

At the time, Herbert Hoover, a Republican, was president of the United States. Unfortunately, his administration was unable to alleviate the crisis, and it fell to his successor, Franklin D. Roosevelt, a Democrat, to do mortal combat with the emergency. Roosevelt's solution was a series of legislative acts and social programs known collectively as the New Deal. According to Rex Tugwell, one of the chief administrators of these programs:

> A new deal [for the American people] was absolutely inevitable. People will submit to grave privations and will even starve peaceably, if they realize that actual dearth exists, but no man . . . will starve in the presence of abundance. The possibility of revolution, either peaceful or violent, against any system which denies the visible means of life to those who have produced those means, will always be with us. Therefore, the only choice before the American people . . . was whether their revolution should follow the course of violence and destruction or should express itself in orderly, legal channels. The answer was given in November 1932, when the American people gave to President Roosevelt a peaceful mandate to attempt to devise a better means of distributing the national income than had previously existed.[3]

The onset of the Great Depression and subsequent implementation of Roosevelt's "peaceful revolution"—the New Deal—changed the United States forever. As noted historian William Leuchtenburg says, these landmark events marked

> one of the turning points of American history. Even at the time, men were aware of a dividing line. In ordinary conversation in the thirties, people would begin by saying "Since '29," or "In the days before the crash.". . . The six years from 1933 through 1938 marked a greater upheaval in American institutions than in any similar period in our history, save perhaps for the impact on the South of the Civil War. [This upheaval can be generally described as] the "Roosevelt Rev-

olution". . . . the devastation wrought by the depression and the remarkable improvisation of new political and social institutions to cope with it.[4]

The Nation's Woes

Leuchtenburg's use of the word "improvisation" to describe the Roosevelt administration's New Deal policies and programs is apt. The scope of the emergency that gripped the country and the world between 1929 and 1933 was so great that no one, not even the best economists of the day, knew exactly how to remedy it, so Roosevelt and his advisors and supporters saw no choice but to improvise. Simply put, they tried attacking the depression on many fronts with a wide array of programs, most of them experimental to one degree or another, hoping that at least some would work.

To grasp the sheer size of the task the Roosevelt administration faced when it came to power in 1933, one must first understand just how devastating the depression actually was for most Americans. Unemployment rates, which had wavered at about 3 percent before October 1929, rose to 9 percent by early in 1930. And in the next two years this rise continued to a crippling 25 percent. (This was the overall rate; as many as half of all black Americans were jobless.) Between the time of the stock market crash and the end of Hoover's presidential term in early 1933, more than nine thousand U.S. banks failed and closed their doors. Some four thousand of these, with combined deposits of $3.6 billion, closed in the first two months of 1933 alone. Because depositors had no insurance to back up their money, millions of Americans lost their entire life savings in a fleeting, tragic instant.

These financial setbacks proved only the beginning of the nation's woes. With the stock market and banks disabled, many businesses went into a fatal tailspin. In 1930, 26,355 U.S. businesses failed, a debilitating figure that was exceeded the following year when 28,285 more went under. The corporations that were still in business in 1932 had a combined deficit of $5.64 billion, a staggering figure at the time; in that same year the nation's volume of manufacturing was only 54 percent of what it had been before the 1929 crash.

Dire Personal Tales

Although these figures illustrate the great scope of the crisis, mere numbers cannot convey the toll of hardships and suffering endured by individuals and families across the land. Their personal tales are much more illustrative and powerful. In May 1932, the executive secretary of a major Philadelphia relief operation reported to Congress the following dire stories:

> One woman said she borrowed 50 cents from a friend and bought stale bread for 3½ cents per loaf, and that is all they [her family] had for eleven days except for one or two meals. With the last food order another woman received she bought dried vegetables and canned goods. With this she made a soup and whenever the members of the family felt hungry they just ate some of the soup. . . . One woman went along the docks and picked up vegetables that fell from the wagons. Sometimes the fish vendors gave her fish at the end of the day. On two different occasions, the family was without food for a day and a half.[5]

No less pitiful was this story filed by a newspaper reporter after visiting North Dakota:

> Last winter the temperature went down to 40 below zero and stayed there for ten days, while a 60-mile wind howled across the plains. And entering that kind of winter we have between 4,000 and 5,000 human beings . . . without clothing or bedding, getting just enough food to keep them from starving. No fuel. Living in houses that a prosperous farmer wouldn't put his cattle in. . . . They now have 850 families on relief, and applications are coming in at a rate of 15 or 20 a day.[6]

A tenement dweller in East Harlem, New York, described a similar plight, writing to his congressman, "It is now seven months I am out of work. . . . I have four children who are in need of clothes and food. . . . My daughter who is eight is very ill and not recovering. My rent is [over]due two months and I am afraid of being put out [evicted]."[7] In another part of New York City, struggling songwriter Yip Harburg testified:

> I was walking along the street . . . and you'd see the bread

lines . . . fellows with burlap on their shoes were lined up all along Columbus Circle, and went for blocks and blocks around the park, waiting. . . . . The prevailing greeting at that time, on every block you passed, by some poor guy coming up, was: "Can you spare a dime?" Or: "Can you spare something for a cup of coffee?". . ."Brother, Can You Spare a Dime?" finally hit on every block, on every street.[8]

Harburg turned that plaintive phrase into what became a sort of Great Depression anthem with which nearly everyone identified. Its sad refrains went in part:

They used to tell me I was building a dream
With peace and glory ahead
Why should I be standing in line
Just waiting for bread? . . .
Say, don't you remember, they called me Al
It was Al all the time
Say, don't you remember I'm your Pal!
Buddy, can you spare a dime?[9]

The Dispossessed

Few could spare even a dime to help American farmers, who were among the hardest hit, especially in the first few years of the crisis. Particularly desperate were the farmers and rural residents of the area encompassing large adjacent tracts of Oklahoma, Texas, Colorado, New Mexico, and Kansas and smaller parts of a few other states. This area became known as the "Dust Bowl" because a severe drought in the 1930s caused much of the light topsoil to blow away, often forming monstrous dust storms. More than half the area's population fled between 1934 and 1937, many heading to California to find harvesting work on large farms there. Noted American writer John Steinbeck captured the migrants' plight in this moving excerpt from his classic novel *The Grapes of Wrath*:

And then the dispossessed were drawn west—from Kansas, Oklahoma, Texas, New Mexico; from Nevada and Arkansas families, tribes, dusted out, tractored out. Carloads, caravans, homeless and hungry; twenty thousand and fifty thousand and a hundred thousand and two hundred thousand. They streamed over the mountains, hungry and restless. . . . The kids are hungry. We got no place to live. Like ants scurrying for work, for food, and most of all for land. . . . And the dispossessed, the migrants, flowed into California, two hundred and fifty thousand, and three hundred thousand. Behind them. . . [other] tenants were being forced off [their lands]. And new waves were on the way, new waves of the dispossessed and the homeless, hardened, intent, and dangerous.[10]

Not surprising, the lost jobs, evictions, breadlines, forced migrations, and other depredations drove many homeless or hopeless Americans to desperate measures, and sometimes even the brink of suicide. Joseph L. Heffernan, the mayor of Youngstown, Ohio, during the depression's early years, recalled one of the distraught jobless men who came to him begging for work:

One man I had known for years stood at my desk and calmly said, "My wife is frantic. After working at the steel mill for twenty-five years, I have lost my job, and I'm too old to get other work. If you can't do something for me, I'm going to kill myself.[11]

Fortunately, the man Heffernan described did not end up taking his own life. But many other desperate individuals did. "This depression has got me licked," went the suicide note of a Houston mechanic.

There is no work to be had. I can't accept charity and I am too proud to appeal to my kin or friends, and I am too honest to steal. So I see no other course. A land flowing with milk and honey and a first class mechanic can't make an honest living. I would rather take my chances with a just God than with unjust humanity.[12]

Mutual Self-Help the Solution?

Until Roosevelt assumed office in 1933, the federal government's response to this overwhelming national crisis was, on the whole, inadequate. In large degree this stemmed from the conservative attitude of the top leaders, beginning with President Hoover (served 1929–1933). They believed it would be unseemly and dangerous for the federal government to provide massive free aid, or "government charity," and that the best approach to alleviating the crisis was to rely on the strength of Americans to help themselves, aided by private charities and state and local relief efforts. Noted historian T.H. Watkins explains:

This was . . . the very ethos of a white, Protestant culture, the image that Hoover and his kind held up as the ideal of Americanism. Hard work, honesty, and independence, they believed utterly, had brought this country to the forefront of nations, had built a breed of men (and women, too, some conceded, though not often) who had taken the institutions of the founding fathers and made them the wonder of the world. Anything that might weaken the strength of that tradition would weaken the very character of America and was, by definition, evil. Government charity, especially, by robbing people of initiative, would be the very embodiment of error. The national government should stay out of the personal lives of its citizens, even if they were in trouble.[13]

Expressing this philosophy in a February 1931 press statement, Hoover stated:

This is not an issue as to whether people shall go hungry or cold in the United States. It is solely a question of the best method by which hunger and cold shall be prevented. It is a question of whether the American people . . . will maintain the spirit of charity and mutual self help . . . as distinguished . . . from appropriations out of the Federal Treasury for such purposes. . . . If we break down this sense of responsibility and individual generosity . . . in times of national difficulty and if we start appropriations of this character we have . . . impaired something infinitely valuable in the life of the American people. . . . Once this has happened . . . we are faced with the abyss of reliance in future upon government charity in one form or another. . . . I am confident that our people have the resources, the initiative, the courage, the stamina and the kindliness of spirit to meet this situation in the way they have met their problems over generations.[14]

Despite this attitude, Hoover and his administration must be credited with an earnest, if highly limited, effort to halt the economic downslide. The most significant part of that effort was the creation early in 1932 of the Reconstruction Finance Corporation (RFC), whose mission was to loan money to failing banks, railroads, insurance companies, and other big businesses. The theory was that if these institutions became solvent, they would put people back to work and thereby stimulate the economy. As Hoover's secretary of the treasury, Ogden Mills, stated it, "I want to break the ice by lending to industry so that somebody will begin to spend in a big way."[15] The RFC did save many businesses and was also helpful when it began loaning money to individual states late in 1932. But it was the only major federal program created to combat a crisis of epic proportions, and by itself it was simply not enough.[16]

Fighting Fear of "Fear Itself"

While the Hoover administration failed to take large-scale action against the ravages of the Great Depression, Roosevelt's regime initiated what could fairly accurately be termed a tidal wave of antidepression legislation. Franklin D. Roosevelt was a fifth cousin of the twenty-sixth president, Theodore Roosevelt (served 1901–1909). The younger Roosevelt, who became known as FDR, had gained notoriety as assistant secretary of the navy during World War I and as a vice presidential candidate in the election of 1920.[17] Soon after losing that race, he suffered a more tragic loss—that of the use of his legs in a bout with polio; however, in an impressive display of courage and determination he reentered politics, serving as governor of New York during Hoover's presidential term. Running against Hoover in the 1932 campaign, Roosevelt won a landslide, garnering 472 electoral votes to the incumbent's 59.[18]

Roosevelt thought that the nation's economic crisis could be alleviated only by the government's taking a fresh approach. He had not revealed the huge scope of his plans during the course of the campaign. But listening to his inaugural address, delivered on March 4, 1933, the American people began to realize that the country was about to undergo a major change of direction. Dropping the usual political and feel-good rhetoric of such speeches, Roosevelt leveled with his countrymen in the opening lines. "This is a day of national consecration," he said in sober, stirring tones, "and I am certain that my fellow-Americans expect . . . [that] I will address them with a candor . . . which the present situation of our nation impels. This is preeminently the time to speak the truth, the whole truth, frankly and boldly." It was time for a change of attitude, he said, for facing and conquering the nervous, gnawing fear of the unknown that presently gripped the country. "The only thing we have to fear is fear itself—nameless, unreasoning, unjustified terror which paralyzes needed efforts to convert retreat into advance." How could that conversion be accomplished? By "treating the task as we would treat the emergency of a war," he asserted.

We must act, and act quickly. . . . If we are to go forward we must move as a trained and loyal army willing to sacrifice for the good of a common discipline, because, without such discipline, no progress is made, no leadership becomes effective. . . . I am prepared under my constitutional duty to recommend the measures that a stricken nation in the midst of a stricken world may require. . . . I shall . . . wage a war against the emergency as great as the power that would be given to me if we were in fact invaded by a foreign foe.[19]

The day after Roosevelt's speech, noted American humorist Will Rogers expressed the hopeful feelings the president's words had instilled in a majority of Americans: "America hasn't been as happy in three years as they are today. No money, no banks, no work, no nothing, but they know they got a man in there who is wise to Congress, wise to our so-called big men. The whole country is with him."[20]

The Hundred Days and Beyond

Soon afterward, the new president revealed the legislative weapons he planned to use in his war against the Great Depression, and it was clear that his measures would go far beyond those of the Hoover administration. The strategy of the New Deal was to attack the crisis forcefully on a number of fronts. In contrast to Hoover's conservative approach, in which government played a minimal role, Roosevelt called for direct and vigorous intervention by the federal government in revitalizing businesses, creating new jobs, providing food and other relief for the needy, and instituting dramatic system-wide reforms.

Roosevelt's opening salvo against the depression came on March 6, just two days after he had assumed office. Summoning a special session of Congress, the president delivered his proposal for a national "bank holiday," in which all banks would close down and show their books to federal inspectors. Based on their assessments, the government would extend emergency aid to those banks that needed it, and only those whose finances were sound would be allowed to reopen. That nearly all of the legislators were ready and willing to try such a bold and unprecedented move is revealed by how speedily they passed it. Without even taking time to read the whole bill, the members of the House of Representatives approved it by a voice vote; a couple of hours later, the Senate passed it almost unanimously; and it reached Roosevelt's desk for his signature only seven hours after he had submitted it, the fastest passage of a legislative bill in U.S. history. The bill's psychological effects on the country seemed almost as swift. With this one sweeping gesture, the president ended the national banking crisis and restored public confidence in the country's banks. About a week after declaring the bank holiday, he wrote to an old friend, "We seem to be off to a good start and I hope to get through some important legislation while the feeling of the country is so friendly."[21]

These words turned out to be an understatement of the first magnitude. The first three months of Roosevelt's first term, now commonly called the historic "Hundred Days," witnessed one of the most ambitious and constructive spurts of presidential-congressional activity in American history. "In the face of an unprecedented national economic crisis, Roosevelt managed to bend the legislature to his will. Congress became almost literally his rubber stamp as he submitted and saw passed into law one sweeping legislative bill after another. Never before or since did a U.S. president hold such commanding authority or enjoy the backing of so many diverse groups of Americans."[22]

Many Far-Reaching Programs

The first major New Deal programs Roosevelt enacted, both of which proved largely successful, were the Agricultural Adjustment Act (AAA), submitted to Congress on March 16, and the Civilian Conservation Corps (CCC), presented on March 21. The AAA was designed to increase the profits of poor farmers by having them reduce production of wheat, corn, rice, and other crops. The theory was that if these foodstuffs became a bit more scarce they would be worth more, so their prices would increase a little, putting more money in farmers' pockets. The CCC's goal was to provide work for the many jobless young men between the ages of eighteen and twenty-five. Between 1933 and 1941, the CCC paid some 2.7 million Americans to plant trees, build dams, fight forest fires, and so on, giving them skills and the means to support their families while helping to reduce the unemployment rate.

One of the New Deal's most far-reaching programs, one that affects nearly all American wage earners and retirees to this day, was the Social Security Act, signed into law on August 14, 1935. The purpose of Social Security was and remains to aid citizens who are in need because of increasing age, unemployment, or sickness. Contributions from both employers and wage earners go into a fund that distributes the money to people over the age of 65, temporarily out of a job, or too ill to work. "We can never insure one hundred percent of the population against one hundred percent of the hazards . . . of life," commented Roosevelt at the signing ceremony, "but we have tried to frame a law which will give some measure of protection to the average citizen and to his family against the loss of a job and against poverty-ridden old age." The law was also a cornerstone in the growing system of New Deal programs, he added, a system "intended to lessen the force of possible future depressions."[23]

Another of Roosevelt's bold and far-reaching programs was the Tennessee Valley Authority (TVA), one of the most ambitious construction projects in world history. The goal was to build fifteen huge dams in the Tennessee River Valley. The benefits would be threefold: to provide millions of Americans with cheap electricity; to help control damaging floods that periodically ravaged the area; and to create years of work for tens of thousands of people. One of the TVA's directors, David E. Lilienthal, later offered this somewhat poetic overview of its accomplishments:

> This is the story of a great change. . . . It is a tale of a wandering and inconstant river now become a chain of broad and lovely lakes which people enjoy, and on which they can depend in all seasons. . . . It is the story of how waters once wasted and destructive have been controlled and now work, night and day, creating electric energy to lighten the burden of human drudgery. Here is a tale of fields . . . [grown] vigorous with new fertility . . . of forests now protected and refreshed . . . of people and how they have worked to create a new valley.[24]

Building, revitalization, and jobs were also major themes of Roosevelt's Public Works Administration (PWA).[25] This federal agency contracted with private companies to construct school and college buildings, hospitals, roads, bridges, sewage systems, and other public works in all but three of the nation's 3,073 counties. By 1939, the PWA had employed about half a million workers per year and financed 34,508 projects at a total cost of about $6 billion. All of these projects were worthwhile and useful thanks largely to the tireless efforts of the agency's scrupulously honest director, Harold L. Ickes, Roosevelt's secretary of the interior.

The Other Side of the Coin: The New Deal's Failures

Like the president, Ickes dreamed and planned on a grand scale and wanted to do far more—for instance, to clear all the nation's slums, to build superhighways from ocean to ocean, and to erect affordable housing for everyone who needed it. There existed at the highest levels of government the feeling that the New Deal might not only end the depression, but also create a new, infinitely better country. In October 1934, Ickes recorded in his diary that Roosevelt

> has great imagination and I told him the other day when I was lunching with him that if he had been president at the time when the Treasury was overflowing, he would have gone down in history as the greatest builder since the world began. He probably will anyhow if we go ahead with such a program as we are discussing.[26]

But despite many sweeping and constructive achievements, Roosevelt, Ickes, and other leading New Dealers often tended to dream bigger than they could deliver. Roosevelt did not become the "greatest builder," for although the CCC, TVA, PWA, and a number of other programs enjoyed varying degrees of success, the other side of the coin revealed that some New Deal efforts were failures. One notable example was the Civil Works Administration (CWA). "Begun in October 1933, the program was designed to put as many Americans to work as possible in the shortest amount of time. At first, it seemed to be on the right track. By January 1934, the CWA had more than 4.2 million people on its employment rolls; but the problem with the program was that it was too unstructured. A lot of people were receiving federal money for questionable or trivial endeavors—raking leaves, for example—and Roosevelt himself saw that the potential existed for creating a class of 'reliefers' who might become perpetually dependent on the government."[27] Accordingly, he admitted his mistake—a rare move for a politician—and closed down the CWA in April 1934.

The New Deal was not, therefore, the ultimate panacea for the nation's economic woes that Roosevelt would have liked it to be. In spite of some real gains, the country's financial recovery was slow and unsteady. It was also at times highly selective. Some groups, particularly minorities, and most notably black Americans, had *two* obstacles to their getting ahead—economic bad times and ingrained prejudice;

not surprisingly, governmental programs that helped many white people gave nonwhites only very limited relief. For example, according to one of Roosevelt's critics, black writer John P. Davis, TVA officials excluded blacks from living in Norris, Tennessee, a model town built to house the workers on Norris Dam. Moreover, Davis pointed out in 1935,

> the [TVA's] payroll of Negro workers remains disproportionately lower than that of whites. While the government has maintained a trade school to train workers on the project, no Negro trainees have been admitted. Nor have any meaningful plans matured for the future of the . . . Negro workers who in another year or so will be left without employment, following completion of work on the dams being built by TVA. . . . None of the officials of TVA seems to have the remotest idea of how Negroes in the Tennessee Valley will be able to buy the cheap electricity which TVA is designed to produce.[28]

In addition, some Americans continued to believe, along with Hoover and most Republican leaders, that Roosevelt's "big government" approach to recovery was immoral, wrongheaded, and dangerous. "The people know now the aims of this New Deal philosophy of government," Hoover stated during the 1936 election campaign (in support of Republican candidate Alf Landon).

> We [the Republican opposition] propose instead leadership and authority in government within the moral and economic framework of the American system. . . . We propose to demobilize and decentralize all this spending upon which vast personal power is being built. . . . The New Dealers say that all this that we propose is a worn-out system; that this machine age requires new measures for which we must sacrifice some part of the freedom of men. Men have lost their way with a confused idea that governments should run machines.[29]

The Ultimate Public Works Project?

These Republican proposals were not enacted, for Roosevelt and the Democrats won the 1936 election (and the 1940 and

1944 elections as well) and the New Deal remained firmly in place. Exactly how much it contributed to the eventual national recovery is difficult to say. In the early 1940s, the country entered World War II, and the economy became supercharged by the enormous avalanche of U.S. war production that turned out to be the largest single factor in the Allied defeat of Germany, Italy, and Japan. As scholar John C. Chalberg remarks, "In the final analysis, the American defense industry proved to be the ultimate public works project."[30]

Thus, the philosophy and overall effectiveness of the New Deal remains somewhat controversial. New Deal critics contend that Roosevelt conducted a large, expensive, and ineffective experiment that continually failed to balance the federal budget, greatly increased the national debt, and built a huge, unwieldy bureaucracy. Roosevelt's defenders counter that the New Deal helped nearly to double national income in its first seven years; employed millions of jobless, desperate people; and, most important, restored the country's morale, which had reached an all-time low during the depression's early years. What these conflicting views show, remarks scholar Mario Einaudi, "is the sharpness of the disputes created by the crisis and the immensity of the issues left in its wake."[31]

However, a majority of modern scholars, while admitting the New Deal was far from perfect, tend to agree with the highly regarded American historian Samuel E. Morison, who wrote:

Franklin D. Roosevelt's administration saved twentieth-century American capitalism by purging it of gross abuses and forcing an accommodation to the larger public interest. This historian, for one, believes him to have been the most effective American conservative since Alexander Hamilton. . . . As Roosevelt remarked in a fireside chat of 1938, democracy had disappeared in certain European nations because their governments said, "We can do nothing for you." But "We in America know that our democratic institutions can be preserved and made to work." And to this task of providing security without impairing fundamental liberties, Roosevelt devoted his major peacetime energies. . . . In 1940, when it became doubtful whether liberty or democracy could survive overt attempts by totalitarian states to conquer the world, it was of utmost importance to mankind that the American democracy weathered the Great Depression and emerged strong and courageous.[32]

Notes

1. *Franklin D. Roosevelt: Portrait of a Great Man.* New York: William Morrow, 1967, pp. 119–20.

2. European countries depended a great deal on American credit, and when that credit became nearly worthless, trade between Europe and North America suffered. In this and other ways, the economies of the United States and most European nations, as well as the other countries with which Europe traded, were so closely linked that the economic upheaval in America inevitably affected everyone.

3. "America Takes Hold of Its Destiny," quoted in William Dudley, ed., *The Great Depression: Opposing Viewpoints.* San Diego: Greenhaven Press, 1994, pp. 113–14.

4. *Franklin D. Roosevelt and the New Deal, 1932–1940.* New York: Harper and Row, 1963, pp. xii-xiii.

5. Quoted in Dudley, *The Great Depression*, p. 36.

6. Quoted in T.H. Watkins, *The Great Depression: America in the 1930s.* Boston: Little, Brown and Company, 1993, p. 125.

7. Quoted in Howard Zinn, *A People's History of the United States.* New York: HarperCollins, 1980, p. 379. The threat of eviction was very real. In 1932 alone, approximately 230,000 American families were forced from their homes for nonpayment of rent.

8. Quoted in Studs Terkel, *Hard Times: An Oral History of the Great Depression.* New York: Random House, 1970, p. 20.

9. "Brother, Can You Spare a Dime?" (1932). Words by E.Y. Harburg, music by Jay Gorney. Quoted in Diane Ravitch, ed., *The American Reader: Words That Moved a Nation.* New York: HarperCollins, 1990, p. 270.

10. New York: Viking Press, 1939, pp. 317–18.

11. "The Hungry City: A Mayor's Experience with Unemployment," in Dudley, *The Great Depression*, pp. 34–35.

12. Quoted in Anthony J. Badger, *The New Deal: The Depression Years, 1933–1940.* New York: Farrar, Straus, and Giroux, 1989, p. 11. The national suicide rate rose from 14 per 100,000 in 1929 to 17.4 per 100,000 in 1932. The rate was much higher in many cities; in Minneapolis, for instance, it peaked at 26.1 per 100,000 in 1932.

13. Watkins, *The Great Depression*, p. 61.

14. Quoted in William S. Myers and Walter H. Newton, *The Hoover Administration: A Documented Narrative.* New York: Charles Scribner's Sons, 1936, pp. 63–64.

15. Quoted in Badger, *The New Deal*, p. 48.

16. The RFC survived the transition to Roosevelt's administration and, when combined with other strong federal programs, became a powerful tool in the na-

tional recovery. Under the direction of Roosevelt's appointee, Texas banker Jesse Jones, the RFC used many of its funds to buy banks' stocks, rather than simply to lend them money. This approach expanded their credit and capital rather than their debt and thereby gave them more financial stability.

17. Roosevelt ran with James W. Cox on the Democratic ticket, which lost the election to the Republican team of Warren G. Harding and Calvin Coolidge.

18. The popular vote was 22.8 million to 15.7 million. The Democrats also captured both houses of Congress, winning the House by 310 to 117 and the Senate by 60 to 35.

19. "First Inaugural Address," in Richard Hofstadter, ed., *Great Issues in American History: A Documentary Record.* vol. 2: *1864–1957.* New York: Vintage Books, 1960, pp. 352–57.

20. Quoted in Samuel Eliot Morison, *The Oxford History of the American People.* New York: Oxford University Press, 1965, p. 950.

21. "Letter of March 13, 1933 to John S. Lawrence," in Elliot Roosevelt, ed., *FDR: His Personal Letters, 1928–1945.* 2 vols. New York: Duell, Sloan, and Pearce, 1950, vol. 1, pp. 338–39.

22. Don Nardo, *Franklin D. Roosevelt: U.S. President.* New York: Chelsea House, 1996, pp. 59–60.

23. "Presidential Statement Upon Signing the Social Security Act, August 14, 1935," in Samuel I. Rosenman, ed., *The Public Papers and Addresses of Franklin D. Roosevelt.* 13 vols. New York: Russell and Russell, 1969, vol. 4, p. 324.

24. Quoted in Richard Hofstadter et al., *The United States: The History of a Republic.* Englewood Cliffs, NJ: Prentice-Hall, 1957, p. 666. By the beginning of World War II, the TVA was producing 2 billion kilowatt-hours of electricity for 83 municipally owned utility companies in Tennessee and neighboring states. Eventually, the project generated over 12 billion kilowatt-hours, not only providing affordable power for homes and businesses, but also making possible the country's massive production of aluminum for ships, vehicles, and weapons in the war.

25. Although they were separate programs, $50 million in PWA funds helped to finance the TVA's dam-building efforts.

26. *The Secret Diary of Harold L. Ickes: The First Thousand Days, 1933–1936.* New York: Simon & Schuster, 1954, p. 206.

27. Nardo, *Franklin D. Roosevelt,* p. 74.

28. "A Black Inventory of the New Deal," in *The Crisis* (1935), quoted in Dudley, *The Great Depression,* p. 189.

29. "Challenge to Liberty Speech of October 30, 1936," in Hofstadter, *Great Issues in American History,* pp. 359–60.

30. "Introduction," in Dudley, *The Great Depression,* p. 21.

31. *The Roosevelt Revolution.* New York: Harcourt, Brace, 1959, pp. 48–49.

32. Morison, *Oxford History of the American People,* p. 987.

Chapter 1

The Origins and Onset of the Great Depression

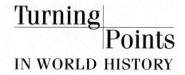

The Stock Market Crash

James D. Horan

As told here by James D. Horan, a prolific chronicler of American history (including *The Wild Bunch* and *The Great American West*), the New York stock market crashed unexpectedly in a time of apparent prosperity. Horan, who, along with his wife, witnessed this traumatic event firsthand, provides a lively overview of the crash itself and some of its immediate effects on American society.

By the fall of 1929 most Americans had climbed the peak of Prosperity high enough to glimpse an unlimited plain in the distance glittering with motor cars, bathtubs, refrigerators, and console radios—the touchstones of progress in their age. It was a time of plenty. Only a year before, President Herbert Hoover had predicted that the day would soon come when poverty in the United States would be abolished for all time.

A Time of Plenty?

The country was at the height of a great industrial development which had begun shortly after the end of the Civil War. Mass production was in high gear. The middle classes were literally at the bursting point after absorbing an unprecedented quantity of worldly goods; it was a lavish era of silk shirts and two-car garages.

The advertisement-bloated Sunday newspapers that fall reflected the nation's prosperity. Custom cars were selling for $10,000 and a man with the right connections could lease a Park Avenue apartment fitted with gold-plated faucets for a trifling $45,000. The market was booming; there were hundreds of thousands, perhaps millions, of new stockhold-

Excerpted from James D. Horan, *The Desperate Years* (New York: Bonanza Books, 1962). Copyright 1962 by James D. Horan.

ers, including clerks, housewives, and truck drivers, and almost every one of them was making profits—on paper. Very few were taking their profits; most of the stock-buying was on margin. But no one worried, certainly not the small investors who had taken most of their savings out of the bank or mortgaged all they owned for cash to play the market. Taxi drivers paid as much attention to the stock quotations from Wall Street as to the score in the afternoon ball game.

In every town in America the Babbitts were keeping up with the Joneses. If they didn't have the cash on hand, they used the installment plan. Before the decade was finished, ten million Americans were paying off debts by the month.

It was true that after Christmas of 1928, there had been a slackening of luxury-item sales. The new cars weren't moving as fast as they had been. Gleaming, oak-boxed radios cluttered display windows. Warehouses began to be jammed. This led to layoffs. Yet this slight tremor in the nation's economy was not felt nationally. Manufacturers read reports of overloaded depots and warehouses and shrugged; it was only temporary, it would soon clear up.

The First Hammer-Blow

Early in September the stock market reached an all-time high. Two days later there was a break, and in the following weeks a gradual slide. But each time the drop seemed to be getting really bad, support came into the market. Then, on the afternoon of October 24, 1929, the first hammer-blow smashed down on this uncomprehending, surfeited, arrogantly self-comfortable world. A total of 12,894,650 shares swamped the board and rocked the financial district. Hysteria swept through Wall Street like a wind-fanned prairie fire. Brokers collapsed under the strain of trying to keep up with orders to sell.

Huge crowds watched the arrival that afternoon of the titans of Wall Street at the House of Morgan. There were the country's top five bankers: Charles E. Mitchell, chairman of the board of the National City Bank; Albert H. Wiggin, chairman of the board of the Chase National Bank; William Potter, chairman of the board of the Guaranty Trust Company; Seward Prosser, chairman of the board of the Bankers Trust Company; and Thomas W. Lamont, senior partner of J.P. Morgan & Co. For a brief few days it seemed as if these giants of finance, shoulder to shoulder, had averted disaster. After the meeting Lamont issued a cheery statement: "There has been a little distress selling on the stock market. . . . There are no houses in difficulty and reports from brokers indicate that margins are being maintained satisfactorily." He added that it was the consensus of the bankers that "many of the quotations on the Stock Market Exchange do not fairly represent the situation."

Yet it had been a hectic, frightening day. The break had been one of the wildest in the market's history, although the losses at the tapping of the three o'clock bell were not particularly large, many having been recouped by an afternoon rally.

The plunge had carried down with it speculators, big and little, in every part of the country, wiping out thousands of accounts. The *New York Times* reported that, had it not been for the calming influence of the five bankers and the subsequent rally, "the business of the country would have been seriously affected." But the wild afternoon had generated many rumors, many of them false. All that afternoon reporters at police headquarters were busy checking with the downtown precincts, trying to confirm a report that eleven brokers had stepped out of windows to their deaths. By five o'clock tension had mounted to such a pitch that a workman outside the upper floor of a Wall Street building found himself staring into the wild eyes of four policemen who were reaching out to pull him inside.

"Don't jump," one cop shouted. "It's not that bad."

"Who's going to jump?" the bewildered man asked. "I'm just washing windows!"

Black Tuesday

But five days later, on October 29—Black Tuesday—Wall Street was in a real panic. The stock market had collapsed. Sixteen million shares were tossed overboard on the New York Stock Exchange for whatever price could be obtained. Similarly, many millions of additional shares were sacrificed

Delafield Public Library
Delafield, WI 53018

in other stock markets, from the Curb Market in New York to the exchanges on the Pacific Coast. The drop in values of listed shares represented a loss of 30 to 60 billion dollars; no one could compute it exactly. And it included Jones's $1,500 and old Mrs. Smith's $5,000, the grocer's $2,500 surplus as well as Mr. Vanderfosterfewster's millions. Besides the excruciating loss that could be seen and felt, there was the un-

The Stark Statistics

These figures show the catastrophic decline in value of twelve common stocks and five important crops in the wake of the great stock market crash.

Prices of Common Stocks

	1929		1932	
	Highest	Lowest	Highest	Lowest
American Telephone & Telegraph	310¼	193¼	137⅞	69¾
Cities Service	68½	20	6⅞	1¼
Electric Bond & Share	189	50	48	5
General Electric	403	168⅛	26⅛	8½
General Motors	91¾	33½	24⅝	7⅝
Kreuger & Toll	46⅜	21⅛	(dead)	—
National Cash Register	148¾	59	18¾	6¼
Radio Corporation of America	114¾	26	13½	2½
Remington Rand	57¾	20⅜	7½	1
Sears, Roebuck	181	80	37⅜	9⅞
United States Smelting, Refining & Mining	72⅞	29⅞	22¾	10
United States Steel	261¾	150	52⅝	21¼

Wholesale Prices of Selected Commodities
Annual Averages to Nearest Half-Cent

	1925	1929	1930	1931	1932	1933	1935	1936
Wheat, bushel	$1.435	$1.035	$0.67	$0.40	$0.38	$0.75	$0.83	$1.025
Corn, bushel	0.70	0.80	0.60	0.32	0.315	0.52	0.655	1.05
Raw cotton, pound	0.235	0.19	0.135	0.085	0.065	0.085	0.12	0.12
Wool, pound	1.40	0.985	0.765	0.62	0.46	0.665	0.725	0.88
Tobacco, pound	0.17	0.185	0.13	0.08	0.105	0.13	0.185	0.235

Quoted in Samuel Eliot Morison, *The Oxford History of the American People.* New York: Oxford University Press, 1965, p. 940.

seen, weakening, undermining impact on the financial structure of the country, on the banks, mortgage companies and investment trusts and funds.

The figures mentioned are 1929 figures. The value or purchasing power of the dollar then was at least three times what it is today, and the number of shares listed on the stock exchanges of 1929 was only a fraction of the number listed today. In relation to today's economic picture the loss was the equivalent of 250 to 500 billion dollars. But the damage to confidence was even more costly. The economic life of the country was smothered in gloom. Faith in the wise men of business and finance was shattered. The people asked for reassurance and guidance.

Secretary of Commerce Robert P. Lamont contented himself with listing the gains for 1929 over the previous year and predicted that prosperity would continue "for the long run." He forgot to say how long that run would be.

Nothing Was Secure Anymore

In Washington, it seemed that everyone was whistling in the graveyard.

As the long winter went on, the rate of unemployment rose; factories shut down, one after another, and office staffs were laid off. By March several millions were idle. Within three years there would be 14,500,000 unemployed.

The first impact of the Depression was not felt in the country's wage structure. The earnings of millions were slashed by layoffs and reduced work schedules before wage rates were undermined. It was not until the end of 1930 that wage changes would be noticed. The drop was about one cent an hour from the 1929 average of fifty-nine cents an hour.

In some quarters wage cuts were being advocated, but such a measure was opposed by both government officials and industrial leaders, who hoped that the maintenance of wage-earners' income would help to stabilize the market for consumer products and stimulate an economic recovery. But before the year was out, wage cuts became a reality. According to Bureau of Labor statistics, in 1929 four times as many employers reported wage increases as reported wage reductions; in the latter part of 1930, wage increases were reported by 126 firms, while 900 reported decreases. As a rule, the cuts were 10 per cent. By the end of the year, an industrial worker who had received an annual wage of $1,500 was now getting $1,300.

Retail business was still going strong in the early months of the new year. Lowboy consoles were selling at $119, and a Fifth Avenue store reported a brisk sale of cloth coats "trimmed with Manchurian wolf" for $38.50, while karakul coats were selling at $88. Food prices hadn't changed much: bread was still 7 cents a loaf, beans 10 cents a can—two for 15 on sale—and butter 49 cents a pound. And there were even plenty of buyers for the air-cooled Franklins, which went for $2,585.

But there was a great uneasiness in the land. As time went on, it became clear to the man in the street that the country's leaders in government, finance, and business, had been badly mistaken or were outrageously misleading him. It seemed that nothing was secure any more. You couldn't depend on anyone or anything. One Fifth Avenue minister warned his congregation: "Our day of reckoning is coming near, prepare yourself. . . ."

The Causes of the Stock Market Crash and Depression

Edward R. Ellis

Many conflicting viewpoints and opinions about what caused the stock market crash and the onset of the depression were advanced in the 1930s, and the debate continues today. In this well-informed essay, Edward R. Ellis, a noted journalist who lived through the depression, summarizes these diverse views and makes the point that a combination of some or many of them were likely involved in the onset of hard times. Like many other observers of the depression, however, he emphasizes one factor above all others, namely the maldistribution of wealth—the accumulation of most of the country's wealth in the hands of just a few individuals, leaving the majority of people struggling to make ends meet and vulnerable to the ravages of an unexpected economic disaster.

People laughed when they read in their newspapers of November 7, 1929, about a New York cop who found an escaped parrot shuffling along Fifth Avenue at Eighty-first Street. The parrot was squawking: "More margin! More margin!"

But people did not laugh very long. They wanted an answer to one overriding question: What caused the Crash on Wall Street?

At the time of the Crash, soon thereafter and even down to the present day a variety of explanations were offered to the public. There is nothing surprising about this diversity of opinions. Economics is not an exact science. Stock market operations cannot be reduced to one simple mathematical

Excerpted from Edward R. Ellis, *A Nation in Torment: The Great Depression, 1929–1939* (New York: Capricorn Books, 1970). Copyright 1970 by Edward Robb Ellis.

formula. Whenever [well-known financier] J. Pierpont Morgan had been asked what he thought the market would do, he always replied: "It will fluctuate." This was no wisecrack. Morgan never indulged in wisecracks. He simply described the market's essential trait: It goes up and it goes down. Now, in 1929, it had gone down so fast and far that everyone was bewildered. When they were able to collect their thoughts, when they tried to comprehend this complex and massive event, each saw it through the prism of his own personality and experience.

World War I a Cause?

Calvin Coolidge may have suffered personal remorse but he was not willing to accept public blame. In an article written for the *Saturday Evening Post* the former President listed a variety of factors, then said: ". . . It will be observed that all these causes of depression, with the exception of the early speculation, had their origin outside of the United States, where they were entirely beyond the control of our Government."

President Herbert Hoover offered several explanations of the Crash and the following Depression.

He declared that "our immediate weak spot was the orgy of stock speculation which began to slump in October, 1929." As for speculators themselves, Hoover added that "there are crimes far worse than murder for which men should be reviled and punished." But a second cause, according to the President, was World War I and its aftereffects. Hoover's war hypothesis was publicly attacked by Senator Carter Glass, who growled that the Depression was no more caused by World War I than it was by the "war of the Phoenicians or the conquest of Gaul by Caesar." It was also criticized in private by Harlan F. Stone, then an Associate Justice of the United States Supreme Court and later its Chief Justice.

Hoover then fell back on Coolidge's argument that the chief causes of the Crash and Depression lay outside the United States. This did not square, however, with findings of the impartial Brookings Institution of Washington, D.C., after its experts had studied conditions in twenty-seven nations, including the United States. According to their report, before prosperity ended in the United States, it had been terminated in eight other nations—Canada, Argentina, Brazil, Germany, Finland, Poland, Australia and the Netherlands Indies. The United States entered the Depression at just about the same time as three other nations—Belgium, Italy and Egypt. However, the United States plunged into the Depression *earlier* than fifteen other nations—Great Britain, Switzerland, Holland, Austria, Czechoslovakia, France, Denmark, Norway, Ireland, Yugoslavia, Japan, India, British Malaya, New Zealand and South Africa.

The Republicans to Blame?

Democrats were quick to blame the Depression on the Republicans. Democratic Congressman John Nance Garner of Texas, fated to become the next Vice President of the United States, said of the Republicans: "Their failure to balance the budget of a family of 120,000,000 people is at the very bottom of the economic troubles from which we are suffering."

[New York] Governor Franklin D. Roosevelt's mother lost heavily in the Crash, but he was slow to understand what had happened. As belatedly as December 1, 1929, in a private letter, Roosevelt referred to the debacle as "the recent little flurry downtown." Ten weeks after the collapse on Wall Street the governor issued a rosy report about New York State finances. In October, 1930, Roosevelt spoke of the need for renewed confidence and private investment. Like many others, he did not think the Depression would last very long. Not until months after the Crash did Roosevelt begin to study it in depth. In another private letter he said: "It would be misunderstood if I were to tell the public that I regard the present business slump as a great blessing, for while a nation goes speculation crazy and everybody is employed, the average citizen simply declines to think of fundamental principles."

Much later, when Roosevelt was the Democratic candidate for President, he attacked Hoover in these words: "So I sum up the history of the present administration in four sentences: First, it encouraged speculation and overproduction, through its false economic policies. Second, it attempted to minimize the crash and misled the people as to its gravity. Third, it erroneously charged the cause to other nations of the world. And finally, it refused to recognize and correct the evils at home which it had brought forth; it delayed reform; it forgot reform."

The Democratic Party's official explanation, as spelled out in its next national platform, was that "the chief causes of this condition were the disastrous policies pursued by our government since the World War, of economic isolation, fostering the merger of competitive businesses into monopolies and encouraging the indefensible expansion and contraction of credit for private profit at the expense of the public."

For obvious reasons, the Republicans disagreed, but the next GOP platform did allude to "the orgy of gambling on the stock exchanges, bank failures and consequent loss of confidence."

The System Itself Corrupt?

Socialist leader Norman Thomas said it was unfair to blame the Crash and Depression on President Hoover since no one man was big enough to cause them. According to Thomas, the cause of the crisis lay within the system itself. The Socialist Party platform elaborated on this, saying in part: ". . . We are facing a breakdown of the capitalistic system. This situation the Socialist Party has long predicted. . . . The capitalistic system is now creaking and breaking in every joint. . . . Capitalism is outworn, obsolete, ready for the museum of social history."

Was this radical talk? Perhaps. However, much the same ideas were being entertained and articulated by men and institutions long in the good graces of the captains of finance and industry. "The capitalistic system is on trial." Who said this? Charles G. Ross, chief Washington correspondent for the eminently respectable St. Louis *Post-Dispatch*, who won a Pulitzer Prize in journalism for his long analysis of the Depression. Ross went on to say: "Men who are not afraid to question the wisdom of unrestricted capitalism—which is practically what we have today—are the real conservators of our institutions. The real threat to them comes not from the handful of Communists in our midst but from the conservative extremists who are not willing to yield an inch. There is vastly more danger to the established order from the economic reactionaries in Congress than there is from the so-called radicals."

One freethinking Republican spokesman, Kansas editor and author William Allen White, wrote a biography of Calvin Coolidge that included this comment: "Speculation alone did not create our economic structure in the Coolidge years. The whole business of blame, credit, responsibility or careless impunity in the journey down the rapids to the economic holocaust lies not in any man, not in any group or institution. Given the American ideals of 1921–29, indeed for two or three previous generations, and the resultant development of those ideals in the American mind alone—with or without Calvin Coolidge or the Federal Reserve System or [noted financier and Treasury Secretary] Andrew Mellon—and the New York bankers would have sped inevitably, sooner or later, to the abysm [sic] of catastrophe. For we had what all Christendom had—a Chamber of Commerce complex."

A Host of Proposed Causes

The International Chamber of Commerce blamed the crisis on: (1) overproduction; (2) decline in commodity prices; (3) world agricultural crisis; (4) industrial unemployment; (5) political unrest; (6) partial closing of several world markets, notably China and India; (7) varied bases for monetary circulation; (8) disequilibrium between short- and long-term credits; (9) fall in silver prices; (10) dumping of goods by Soviet Russia; (11) unprecedented taxation to meet international indebtedness; (12) excessive state participation in private enterprises.

The National Association of Manufacturers said that the main factor in the Depression was the misuse of credit, although misdirected government action was also responsible. The reactionary NAM went on to argue that the Federal Reserve System failed to apply credit brakes and that the government encouraged risky foreign loans. Restrictions were continued on the international movement of goods, although we had shifted from a debtor to a creditor nation. However, the NAM concluded, public opinion supported the inflationary policies pursued by business and government.

William Cardinal O'Connell of Boston was himself a conservative, but he declared that the Depression was due to a "ghastly failure of industrial leadership." Treasury Secretary Mellon singled out overproduction as the principal cause of all the trouble. The *Commercial and Financial Chronicle* blamed everything on the Federal Reserve's policy. Congressman Fiorello H. LaGuardia of New York blamed the bankers, crying: "The bastards broke the people's back with their usury!" John L. Lewis, president of the United Mine Workers, agreed with LaGuardia, declaring: "A horde of small-time leaders in industry and finance looted the purse of the population."

Professor Irving Fisher said the disaster was due to "mob psychology" and then added—à la Morgan—that "the market went down because it went down." Bertrand H. Snell, soon to become the Republican minority leader in the House of Representatives, called the Depression "the ghost of the World War stalking over the earth." William Randolph Hearst, the prince of publishers, said the Depression was caused by enormous overcapitalization which had stolen billions from small investors; he also said that "if profits had been distributed in wages, prosperity would have been maintained and increased."

Too Much Wealth in the Hands of a Few?

Governor Roosevelt agreed with Hearst. "Our basic trouble," said Roosevelt, "was not an insufficiency of capital. It was an insufficient distribution of buying power coupled with an over-sufficient speculation in production. While wages rose in many of our industries, they did not rise proportionately to the reward to capital, and at the same time the purchasing power of other great groups of our population was permitted to shrink."

Agreement came from Senator James Couzens of Michigan, a Republican and a multimillionaire. Couzens said:

"Notwithstanding the general assumption that wages were high, all available statistics show that during the years preceding the depression the increase in productivity per man was greater than the increase in wages. In other words, although the worker got more money, he produced still more goods. Somebody got the difference, and we all know who it was."

Capitalists were paid too much. Workers were paid too little. Charles G. Ross said in his prizewinning article: "The wealth created by the machine has gone, in appalling disproportion, to the owners of the machine." Other sources pointed out that 12 executives in the tobacco industry received salaries equivalent to the gross income of 30,000 tobacco farmers and their families. Republican Senator William E. Borah of Idaho said that Bethlehem Steel gained 160 percent in earnings the first six months of 1929, that the Republic Iron and Steel Company showed profits of 208 percent, and the Youngstown Sheet and Tube Company's profits rose 145 percent. Borah might have added that between 1924 and 1929 the steel industry did not grant a single wage increase.

This cynical indifference to the welfare of workers played right into the hands of the Communists. Karl Marx had declared that in the end capitalism would provide "its own grave digger." He claimed to have discerned several trends in capitalism which would inevitably cause its collapse: an incessant urge to accumulate more and more capital; an increasing concentration of the means of production in the hands of fewer and fewer monopolists, accompanied by the ruination of most businessmen; a steady fall in the rate of profit in relation to capital investment; and an increase in the misery of the working class. On the basis of these trends, Marx developed a theory of the business cycle in which each depression would be more disastrous than the last, until finally the last crisis would bring about the collapse of capitalism.

The Roman Catholic Church, which vigorously opposed Communism, nonetheless took a position somewhat similar to that of the Marxists. On May 15, 1931, Pope Pius XI issued an encyclical bearing the title "On Reconstructing the Social Order." In part, the Pope said:

> . . . it is obvious that not only is wealth concentrated in our times but an immense power and despotic economic dictatorship is consolidated in the hands of a few, who often are not owners but only the trustees and managing directors of invested funds which they administer according to their own arbitrary will and pleasure.
>
> This dictatorship is being most forcibly exercised by those who, since they hold the money and completely control it, control credit also and rule the lending of money. Hence, they regulate the flow, so to speak, of the life-blood whereby the entire economic system lives, and have so firmly in their grasp the soul, as it were, of economic life, that no one can breathe against their will. . . .

Governor Huey Long of Louisiana said much the same thing in plain words: "The wealth of the land was being tied up in the hands of a very few men. The people were not buying because they had nothing with which to buy. The big business interests were not selling, because there was nobody they could sell to. One percent of the people could not eat any more than any other one percent; they could not wear much more than any other one percent; they could not live in any more houses than any other one percent. So, in 1929, when the fortune-holders of America grew powerful enough that one percent of the people owned nearly everything, ninety-nine percent of the people owned practically nothing, not even enough to pay their debts, a collapse was at hand."

A Loaded Gun

What caused the Crash?

Greedy people wanted more than they needed. Foolish people thought they could get something for nothing. Impulsive people bought now in the hope of paying later. Income and wealth were distributed unfairly and dangerously. The rich regarded themselves as an all-knowing elite. The masses were not paid enough money to consume all the goods they produced. The economy was unsound. The corporate structure was sick. The banking system was weak. Foreign trade was out of balance. Business data were inadequate and often faulty.

This constellation of conditions left the economy a flawed and loaded gun, and when the stock market crashed, the gun did not merely fire—it exploded in everyone's face.

From *The History of the New Deal, 1933–1938*

Basil Rauch

> Hoover's administration was guided in large degree by the creed of "rugged individualism," which held that the federal government should, whenever possible, stay out of people's lives. Left to its "natural" course, Hoover maintained, the "initiative and enterprise" of individual citizens would surely "spur on the march of progress." As explained here by historian Basil Rauch, a leading scholar of the depression era, because of this creed the measures that Hoover and his advisors instituted to combat the growing economic crisis were far too timid.

Inevitably the depression placed the problems of industry in the center of the political stage. Shortly after the stock market crash a conference of business and labor leaders resulted in promises to maintain wages and production. A special inducement was granted to business in the form of a 1 per cent reduction in income taxes. Unemployment was relieved by expanding the government's public-works program. The administration urged that confidence was the key to the situation.

The response of business to this first attempt to deal with the depression was disquieting. Corporations increased their dividend rates, and new fixed-investment trusts and pool managers worked up a partial restoration of the bull market. But production failed to gain. Consequently, in May, 1930, the stock market crashed again, and a two-year downward spiral of prices and production began. Industry ignored its promises to maintain wages and employment in a desperate effort to cut them faster than prices fell.

Excerpted from *The History of the New Deal, 1933–1938*, by Basil Rauch. Copyright ©1944 and copyright renewed ©1971 by Basil Rauch. Reprinted by permission of Farrar, Straus & Giroux, Inc.

For over a year the President accepted the collapse as an inevitable liquidation of inflated values which should be allowed to run its course. In June, 1930, he signed the Hawley-Smoot Tariff Act, which raised the rates to the highest level in history. Economists had warned him that the new law would deepen the world depression and benefit the protected American interests very little if at all. The President himself had promised to lower the rates, but by 1930 he had decided that the danger of foreign dumping in American markets justified violation of his promise.

In October of that year the President's Emergency Committee on Employment was appointed, with Colonel Arthur Woods, a business leader, as its chairman. The Committee, launched two weeks before the Congressional elections, was widely interpreted as a bid for the labor vote which should commit the administration to nothing more than recognition of the problem. It failed to turn the electoral tide in favor of the administration, and within a few months its chairman had resigned. One labor paper declared that the resignation of Colonel Woods made the "futility" of Hoover's interest in the unemployed "sort of official."

Democratic gains in Congress in the elections of November, 1930, left the Republicans only a minority of members of the House, but did not result in repudiation of the administration's policies. The dominant leadership of the Democrats was in the hands of Eastern conservatives, and they worked with the President's party to pass every important measure for which he asked. Shortly after the November elections, the leaders of the National Democratic Committee, Jouett Shouse and John J. Raskob, assured the President that they would not be partisan, but would stand by even the Hawley-Smoot Tariff.

Only a minority of liberal Democrats in Congress worked with the Western insurgent wing of the Republicans to fight for more thorough-going action by the administration to deal with the depression. They joined in a conference which passed resolutions in favor of unemployment insurance, lower tariff rates, and other liberal measures. Governor Franklin D. Roosevelt sent the conference a message of approval, thus early displaying his support of the liberal rather than the conservative wing of his party, and of the Republican insurgents besides. In Congress this bi-partisan group succeeded in passing a resolution in favor of government operation of the power plant at Muscle Shoals, site of the future Tennessee Valley Authority, but Hoover vetoed it in March, 1931.

The argument which was to be most potent in turning the 1932 election against Hoover—that his administration was interested only in protecting businessmen from the worst effects of the depression—was developed in a debate over drought-relief. Farmers of the plains country were suffering in 1931 from the first of a series of severe droughts which were to turn great areas into a dust bowl. The President proposed that the government lend money to the drought-ridden farmers inasmuch as they were in the position of businessmen who needed credit. The loans were to be made only when secured by property, and were to be used only to restore property values by feeding livestock, buying implements, and otherwise increasing the capital value and money-making potential of farmers' enterprises. It was pointed out by such Western Senators as Caraway and Robinson, however, that farmers were going hungry, and that they could not feed livestock unless they themselves were fed first. The administration countered that it was no part of the duties of the federal government to provide direct relief as gifts in order to relieve human suffering. Such relief should be provided by local private and public agencies. The limit of the federal government's obligation was the provision of loans to relieve credit stringencies in productive enterprises.

It was well understood by both sides that not merely relief for a relatively few farmers, but the administration's policy on relief for the ever-swelling millions of unemployed was being debated. Private charity in even the richest districts was unable to meet the need, and local and state governments were exhausting their credit. The drought-ridden farmers merely presented the problem in the most acute form: local relief was unable to save them from starvation. Nevertheless the administration clung stubbornly to its principle.

Threatened with an extra session of Congress, the President signed a Drought-Relief Bill which appropriated $20,000,000 for loans for seed and for "further agricultural rehabilitation"—a loophole which Secretary of Agriculture Hyde admitted, when pressed by Senator Borah, might possibly be used to provide food for the starving farmers. But the administration did not admit that it was violating its relief policy, and the President promptly vetoed the Wagner Bill to extend the work of federal employment agencies to states which sponsored no agencies of their own, on the ground that it would interfere with state control over unemployment problems.

In 1931, bank failures emphasized the new depths to which the country's economy was descending. The President's efforts to restore confidence by making optimistic statements began to be treated as comic diversions from the realities of life. In a speech at Indianapolis he made a strenuous effort to present his policies in a constructive light. He promised an American "Twenty-Year Plan" for the development of the country's prosperity by judicious federal encouragement of private enterprise through public support of airways, river transport, and land reclamation. But the twenty-year scope of this plan seemed to indicate not so much far-sightedness as timidity in the use of federal power to solve immediate problems. Little more was heard of the plan. Similarly, the President's appeals to Wall Street and the commodity exchanges to stop the short-selling which was depressing prices to unnaturally low levels, appeals to the voluntary good will of operators, seemed timid to the point of absurdity when the President of the New York Stock Exchange, Richard Whitney, told the House Judiciary Committee that the very existence of exchanges depended on short-selling.

In September, 1931, Great Britain went off the gold standard. The President was convinced that deflation had gone far enough. Believing that lack of confidence was driving the process to the point where the banking and money systems were endangered, he determined to act in defense of these last bulwarks.

His first action merely encouraged bankers to help themselves. On October 8, after conferences among the President, Congressmen, and bankers, it was announced that the latter would form a $500,000,000 National Credit Corporation, which would rediscount frozen assets unacceptable to the Federal Reserve Banks and a wide range of assets of banks which were not members of the Federal Reserve. The Corporation was opened for business on November 10. During the interval the President's new Organization on Unemployment Relief had reported that such relaxation of bank credit was the main solution of the unemployment problem.

Less than a month after the National Credit Corporation had been established, the President decided that self-help would not save the banking system. He asked the new Congress to establish the Reconstruction Finance Corporation to lend federal money to banks, insurance companies, railroads, and other key enterprises. Congress complied, and the RFC was set up early in 1932 with capital of $500,000,000 provided by the government and $1,500,000,000 obtained by the sale of notes guaranteed by the government. Many banks and corporations were undoubtedly saved by RFC loans, but deflation was not halted, and within a year a new wave of bank failures could not be prevented.

Meanwhile the RFC was attacked as the final proof that the administration favored bankers and businessmen above other citizens, and great corporations over small businesses. The latter contention seemed valid when the President vetoed the Wagner-Garner Relief Bill which would have extended RFC loans to small businesses and to individuals. This veto was the only administration action which did not square with its principle that loans were within the limits of the government's obligation to any economic group. The administration showed, however, that it was willing to extend the benefits of its credit policy to certain other groups by passing a measure to expand the capitalization of Federal Land Banks, and by establishing Home Loan Banks to lend money on home mortgages. The facts remained that federal action to limit agricultural production was the most pressing need of the farmers, federal action to stop competitive wage-cutting was the most pressing need of employed workers, and direct federal relief was the only means of preventing extreme hardship for the unemployed. And the opinion grew bitter among farmers and laborers that not constitutional rectitude but class favoritism dictated the administration's refusal to meet the most pressing need of any group except big business.

This opinion was increasingly reflected in Congress during the spring of 1932. Liberal Democrats and insurgent Republicans did not deny the administration's duty to combat the depression in the areas it had selected; rather they demanded that similar action be taken in all areas. The Glass-Steagall Bill to broaden acceptability of commercial paper by the Federal Reserve Banks and to release gold formerly held to support currency was passed unanimously, taxes were increased, executive agencies reorganized, and government payrolls cut. After the veto of the Wagner-Garner Relief Bill, it was amended to meet the President's objections, and a provision added for loans to the states for relief, after which it was passed and signed. But a bill to give Congress the President's existing right to make emergency changes in tariff rates and authorizing reciprocity tariff treaties was vetoed. Measures which passed the House but not the Senate to provide expansion of the currency and direct federal unemployment relief were blamed by the President for the failure of business to regain "confidence."

Politically the more significant fact was that revelations by Congressional investigations of malpractices of bankers, utility magnates, and brokers, and the President's failure to adopt any counter-measures, resulted in a rapid ebb of public confidence in both business and the President. While the Chief Executive seemed to lose no measure of his respect for big business, he harried out of Washington with tear gas and fired the war veterans who petitioned for a cash bonus.

A slight upturn in business which began in July offered the President his chief argument for re-election. He and the leaders of his party relied heavily on statistical proofs that the worst was over when active campaigning began in September. The argument failed to still the demands of laborers and farmers for government aid, or to overcome the general impression of the administration's favoritism to big business and its political incompetence.

For months before the presidential election of 1932, the traditional danger signal for an American administration had been flying: the only major sectional-class interest which was united in support of the Hoover administration and the Republican Party was Eastern business, and it was apathetic as well as outnumbered in its own section by laborers and unemployed who wanted a change. The natural beneficiary of the failure of the Hoover administration to hold the loyalty of at least two major sectional-class groups was the Democratic Party. By adding to the votes of the Solid South those of Eastern laborers and unemployed and Western farmers, that party could recreate the great coalition which had elected Jefferson and Wilson. It remained to be seen whether a leader of their stature could be found who would make his election another main turning on the road of American history.

Chapter 2

The Depression's Debilitating Impact

Turning | Points
IN WORLD HISTORY

The Plight of the Cities

John F. Bauman and Thomas H. Coode

It is perhaps not surprising that all American urban centers were hard hit by the depression. This essay about the economic plight of the cities is an excerpt from the informative *In the Eye of the Great Depression,* by John F. Bauman and Thomas H. Coode, professors of history at California University of Pennsylvania. Focusing their narrative through the eyes of reporters who visited the cities in the early 1930s, the authors detail the vast scope of unemployment and poverty, the near futility of relief efforts, the often insensitive attitude of employers, and the growing strains of ethnic and racial prejudice.

America became an urban nation in the 1920s, and American cities became showplaces for the achievements of modern technology and the display of modern marketing principles. In fact, in the popular mind the word *civilization* created images of the modern city with its skyscrapers, paved streets, and palatial department stores which seemingly epitomized the consumption ethic of the New Era society. The Great Depression, however, shattered any illusion that this urban civilization implied unending prosperity, making a mockery of its glitter while underscoring the hazards and trauma popularly associated with city life. . . .

Unlike the earlier depressions which had struck in 1873, 1893, 1914, and again in 1921, the Great Depression of 1929 stalled America's industrial machine and paralyzed her cities. The resources of private voluntarism, which once enabled cities and their jobless to weather cyclic economic storms, failed. Soup kitchens, missions, ward relief organizations, family societies, and ancient poor boards collapsed under the

Excerpted from John F. Bauman and Thomas H. Coode, *In the Eye of the Great Depression* (DeKalb: Northern Illinois University Press). Copyright 1988 by Northern Illinois University Press. Used by permission of the publisher. (Endnotes in the original have been omitted in this reprint.)

weight of mass poverty. Faced with the spectacle of long bread lines, incidents of actual starvation, and the portents of popular insurrection, in 1931 President Herbert Hoover had attempted to coordinate the disparate ranks of voluntary relief, first through the President's Emergency Committee on Employment and then through the President's Organization on Unemployment Relief. Furthermore, seeking to bulwark voluntarism, cities such as Philadelphia appropriated emergency funds, and states like New York established the first state welfare agency, the New York Temporary Emergency Relief Administration (TERA). However, by 1933, with the urban poor scavenging city docks for bits of rotting vegetables, it became clear to social workers, civic leaders, mayors, and economists that without bold federal intervention cities were defenseless against the enormity of the Great Depression.

A Mood of Hopelessness

In 1933 the administration of Franklin Delano Roosevelt became the first in American history to acknowledge the special predicament of the city in a period of economic crisis. Indeed, many of the early New Deal agencies—the National Recovery Administration (NRA), the Federal Housing Administration (FHA), the Home Owners' Loan Corporation (HOLC), and the Federal Emergency Relief Administration (FERA)—were created with the intention of bolstering the faltering urban economy.

As one aspect of this concern for urban America, New Dealers hoped to modernize the creaky, antiquated machinery of city unemployment relief. To that end, [FERA chief] Harry Hopkins instructed his roving investigators to seek information on the size of the urban relief population, the pace of urban industrial recovery, the struggle of the urban jobless to exist, and the effectiveness of federal relief in suppressing what the observers perceived as a rising tide of social disorder and radicalism.

Hopkins dispatched his reporters to all the nation's major cities and to many smaller urban centers as well. Lorena Hickok visited New York, Philadelphia, and Baltimore;

Thomas Steep surveyed Chicago, Milwaukee, and Gary, Indiana; Louisa Wilson and Lincoln Colcord spent time in Detroit, Akron, and other Ohio cities; and Edward Webster studied conditions in St. Louis. At the same time, David Maynard concentrated on Cleveland, Cincinnati, and Indianapolis, and Ernestine Ball on such upstate New York cities as Troy, Jamestown, and Buffalo. In every city the reporters interviewed industrialists, small local businessmen, federal relief officials, local political and civic leaders, social workers, and, of course, the jobless themselves. . . .

Whether the city visited in 1933 and 1934 was a large metropolis such as Philadelphia or New York, an industrial center like Milwaukee or Gary, or a smaller city such as Troy, New York, or Waltham, Massachusetts, Hopkins's reporters were decidedly pessimistic about the future of urban industrialism. Although New Deal emergency measures appeared to be relieving some of the panic which had gripped cities in 1931 and 1932, when hunger marchers invaded the downtowns of urban America, reporters like Hickok demured: "The emergency [may be] over," a Bronx social worker had told her, "but," as Hickok too believed, "the Depression lingers on." Wayne Parrish reinforced this growing impression on one of his several visits to Harlem, East Harlem, and the Queens section of New York. "With no private jobs in sight," Parrish witnessed relief rolls rising steadily in 1934. Among the workers he talked to, Parrish discerned "a complete lack of faith . . . that private jobs [were ever] coming back. Scores of employers had given up their businesses," and of those still operating, "most are willing to take back their people if business picks up; but they are not hopeful."

Perhaps an even darker pall hung over Chicago. . . .

Chicago's Sears and Roebuck Company had increased working hours and reduced its working force by 1,700 employees in 1934. Sears's vice-president of operations told Steep that he saw "no prospect for a pickup. Our calculation is for a decline." When Sears, despite the depression, opened a new retail store in Chicago, a desperate crowd of 6,000 people applied for the 500 jobs. "There had been no advertising for help wanted," a Sears official told Steep.

Chicago's large industrial plants presented equally dismal prospects for reemployment. In November 1934, fewer than 10 percent of the Pullman Car and Manufacturing Company's normal work force of 8,000 were on the job. The company in 1934 operated 4,300 sleeping cars, but in 1929 it had had 8,800 in service. Railroad porters employed by Pullman dropped from 12,000 in 1929 to 8,000 five years later. During the same time, Pullman reduced its complement of conductors from 2,400 to 1,600. Thomas Steep sensed a "graveyard quiet" pervading the Hog Capital of the World. Driving through the streets of Pullman, Steep "did not see half a dozen people and no automobiles. . . . Most of the tenants [are] on relief." He observed that many of the large brick buildings of the Pullman operation were silent, without a single workman visible, and the spaces between the buildings were now filled with an autumn crop of weeds. Steep talked with a plant manager who lamented that he once saw "as many as 13,000 men employed" there, but now, instead of the din of machinery, all was silent, and a somber hopelessness prevailed.

It was perhaps even worse in Chicago's building trades. Of the 30,000 carpenters, 22,000 painters, and 73,000 other members holding cards in the Chicago Building Trades Council, only 10,000 worked regularly. All the others, Steep reported, "live on odd jobs and relief, occupying homes in which two or three families combine and pool their food."

Closed Down for Good

Here, then, in the heart of urban America, Hopkins's reporters discovered a stranded population, superfluous people, apparently adrift in the swirling tides of an urban industrial culture. Assessing the consequences in the 1920s of the efficiency to be gained by industrial modernization, many later New Dealers such as Rexford Tugwell had early reached the solemn conclusion that textile workers and other mechanics engaged in outmoded trades were permanently unemployable. He felt that, like sharecroppers and tenant farmers in rural America, these superfluous laborers contributed to excess production and thus fueled cyclic economic dislocations. In Tugwell's mind the Great Depression vindicated his theory and confirmed the need to resettle these stranded urban populations in rural areas where they could subsist by raising their own food and engaging in small craft enterprises. This belief that urban economies had exhausted their potential for fostering employment opportunity helped stir other early New Deal experiments such as urban garden plots and cooperative enterprises for canning vegetables and manufacturing mattresses. Of course, the most singular outcome of these doubts about the viability of

---

"Buy an Apple"

As told here by historian James D. Horan, one of the most common sights in depression-wracked cities was the roadside apple peddler.

In the fall of 1930 appeared a figure that was to become the symbol of the Depression—the apple-peddler. If you couldn't get a job you could at least sell apples and perhaps make enough to buy a meager meal for yourself and your family. Men who had once been engineers, mechanics, clerks, stockbrokers—men who had once owned homes, cars, and businesses—huddled on street corners and sold their polished apples for a nickel. There usually was a small sign:

BUY AN APPLE.

HELP THE UNEMPLOYED.

Sometimes there were no signs: everyone knew what this man was doing standing beside the box. He was trying to survive.

The main apple depot in New York was the Apple Growers' Association, at West and Harrison streets on Manhattan's lower East Side. Most of the men and women who came there lined up before dawn after a restless night in the Salvation Army's Bowery headquarters, the "Munie" (Municipal Lodging House), or the "cold dock," an infamous East River pier hastily erected as an annex to the "Munie" when the city's unemployment and homeless population began to increase in the latter months of 1930.

James D. Horan, *The Desperate Years.* New York: Bonanza Books, 1962, pp. 13–14.

the urban economy was the Resettlement Administration, which proposed to build a series of planned garden towns along the urban periphery.

Undoubtedly, the evidence from social workers and other observers of urban America in the early 1930s reinforced this grim verdict on the economic future of the city. Among the jobless textile and metal workers of Philadelphia, hope barely flickered. Although the businessmen and civic leaders reporter Julian Claff interviewed believed that the worst was over, none envisioned a bright future for the city. Instead, they predicted that the city's economy would merely "limp along" indefinitely. Businessmen grumbled to him that "labor troubles, heavy taxes, and a rotten city government" had already driven many factories out of Philadelphia, while "others are only too eager for a chance to get out." In his observations, Claff sounded the theme uttered again and again in the reports that "this decentralizing trend stranded many thousands here who will never get work.". . .

In cities with less diversified economies such as Detroit, joblessness and poverty seemed so ubiquitous [widespread] that a mood of unmitigated helplessness enveloped the town. Despite some slight improvement in the automobile industry, in the spring of 1934 Lincoln Colcord described Detroit's economy as still languishing in "a condition of deep depression. . . . Traffic on the downtown streets on weekdays [was] noticeably light. Merchants," Colcord wrote, "report that sales of low priced goods are fairly steady, but these sales are attributed . . . to the underlying support of relief funds. . . . [Detroit] does not seem so much disturbed as it seems prostrated. One gets a clear impression of a community that has suffered so heavily and so long from the Depression that it is almost losing heart."

Colcord labeled America's automobile capital "the spear point of the Depression." But the lance was pierced as deeply into the heart of smaller industrial cities like Gary, Indiana, where in 1934 mills such as Illinois Steel operated at 22 percent of capacity and hosts of smaller plants were shut down entirely. Thomas Steep found the Gary region "dotted with silent factory buildings." One industrial survey he consulted questioned seriously whether most of the thousands of Gary's jobless would ever be reemployed. Steep quoted an employment survey that listed Standard Steel Car Company—"Closed Down for Good"; Hammond Pattern and Foundry—"Closed due to Bank Foreclosure"; and Gary Screw and Bolt—"Closed, No Business." Even those plants that were still operating suffered hard times. For instance, Universal Atlas Cement only employed 350 men out of its normal work force of 1,600 and for the future "did not anticipate . . . ever hiring as many men as it [the company] did in 1929.". . .

Many Uncaring Employers

In all the cities they visited, large and small, the reporters found the horrendous economic conditions exacerbated by a disturbing business-as-usual attitude among the employer class. Many businessmen publicly distrusted the programs and goals of the early New Deal: the federal monetary policy, the work relief projects, national wage scales, and the labor provisions of the National Industrial Recovery Act. Despite the severity of the Great Depression, business interests remained motivated by the lure of profits and in many cases seemed bereft of even the slightest sense of altruism. In Rochester, New York, reporters wrote of a "contented conservatism," the determination of businessmen that "the only danger is that business will lose confidence if the [Roosevelt] Administration makes more concessions to labor or moves further to the left." After a few days in Columbus and Cleveland, Ohio, David Maynard found "plenty of money on hand for business expansion, but industrialists and bankers [are] uninterested in investing because of a lack of confidence about what the government will do next and a general feeling that there is very little chance of profits."

Often, this lack of confidence and conscience manifested itself perniciously in company policy. When Campbell Soup's economic position improved, the company reduced its labor force and sped up the work pace rather than reemploying workers and expanding production. Several examples from Baltimore illustrate . . . business's "lack of confidence." Cynical Baltimore employers converted the National Recovery Administration's minimum wage provision into the standard hourly rate; in other words, the minimum rate became the maximum hourly wage. Department stores in Baltimore paid their clerks "only for the time they actually work[ed] and sen[t] them home during quieter hours." Montgomery Ward there hired waitresses for three hours a day at twenty-five cents an hour, a practice legal under the NRA's Restaurant Code but ruthless on the waitresses, who had to pay twenty cents for streetcar fare to get to work. Then, too, department stores frequently hired the hapless unemployed to peddle electrical appliances door-to-door on a commission-only basis. As Lorena Hickok bitterly observed, "If he sells anything, that's just gravy to the department store." At the same time, Baltimore auto mechanics were paid only while actually working on a car; when not working, they were required to "hang around without pay." As one employer put it: "If they don't like it, [they can] go somewhere else. Plenty of labor available these times!". . .

Saddened by what they saw in these cities, the reporters poignantly reflected upon the social cost of the Great Depression. The American worker had historically been heralded as the bone and sinew of the nation. According to the popularizers of the American Way, it had been the nation's workers, the men who made steel, mined coal, built automobiles, and ran the railroads, who had exchanged their wrenches and drill presses for rifles and defeated the Kaiser in World War I. How completely had the depression obliterated that Bunyanesque [i.e., Paul Bunyan–like] image of the American worker? In 1934, a local social worker told Steep that "the men who have found their efficiency impaired no longer take chances of getting off relief." Elsewhere the jobless wandered as human flotsam drifting from city to city and flopping for months at a time in shelters for homeless men. Julian Claff branded Philadelphia's shelter "a genuine plague spot." All seven hundred residents of the shelter—located in a brick building which had once housed the Baldwin Locomotive Works—"appeared to be fixtures" in Lorena Hickok's eyes. "Nothing more can be done about

them" she reported to Hopkins, "they can't handle themselves any more. They have slipped so far down the scale
that they are content to rest and throw the responsibility on
the flop management, while they spend a little spare time in
digging up an occasional pint of gin." The real crime,
Hickok wrote, was that most of these men were not the usual
municipal flop house denizens. "Once, and not so long ago,
they were citizens."

The Cities Totally Unprepared

For the majority of the jobless, still rooted in family units,
months, even years of joblessness had exhausted their savings
and driven them to seek the cheapest and most dilapidated
housing. Moldering tenement units, once considered unfit
for human habitation, became homes for not one but often
several families who sought any, even the barest excuse for,
shelter. Hickok toured Philadelphia's notorious "bandbox"
slums where the poor were crammed into tiny, box-like,
three-story structures—one 10 by 10 cubicle teetering above
another. These antiquated rookeries lacked not only gas and
electricity but also the plumbing necessary for basic sanitary
facilities. Likewise, Thomas Steep found housing in Gary, Indiana, "pretty terrible. Some buildings are stuffed to suffoca-
tion with clients (the jobless) while hundreds of houses are
empty because they have been taken over by banks and insurance companies and no one can pay the rent asked. . . . As
elsewhere, scores of jobless men who formerly thought they
owned their own homes have been evicted and have judg-
ments hanging over their heads for balances due.". . .

Significantly, the reporters in late 1934 predicted little
abatement of the crisis. After touring St. Louis, Kansas City,
Tulsa, Dallas, and Fort Worth, Edward Webster was more
appalled than ever at "the scale of relief," "the magnitude
and the complexity of the task," and the "disposition of
America to interpret it all with placid fatalism.". . .

During the first years of the Great Depression, American
cities were totally unprepared to deal with mass unemployment in an urban-industrial society. In 1933, for example,
New York City's entire caseload consisted of under half a

million persons whom the city aided at a cost of slightly over $30,000,000. Then, in the first six months of 1934, the city's combined public and private caseload skyrocketed to over 1,500,000 people, whom it now cared for at a staggering cost of $50,524,309. Lorena Hickok termed New York's relief crisis as "breathtaking." One city block she visited housed over 200 relief families.

Like the professional altruists who administered private and public welfare in the city, the reporters regularly bemoaned the inadequacy of urban relief funds and criticized the inefficiency of politically motivated local relief agencies. Not surprisingly, in New York Hickok found lack of money to be the problem which "has been and still is and will continue to tower above all others." Even with the new "triangular system" whereby federal, state, and city governments each contributed a third of the welfare costs, Hickok figured that New York would still require $10,000,000 a month for relief; yet, she reported, the city "ought to be [spending] $15,000,000 a month, and even that would be barely adequate.". . .

The "Deserving" and the "Undeserving"

Who were the thousands of people whose impoverishment and misery overburdened the finite resources of city welfare funds and taxed the ingenuity of Harry Hopkins and the Federal Emergency Relief Administration? According to Hickok, New York City's relief rolls encompassed over thirty nationalities: "Thousands of them," wrote Hickok, "cannot speak a word of English," but, she added, "among them are business and professional men whose incomes five years ago ran into many thousands of dollars."

As can be seen in Hickok's observations, just below the surface of these reports on America's cities there seemed to be an undue preoccupation with the ethnic, racial, and class identity of the unemployed. Unquestionably, the reports embodied an expression of ethnocentrism, symptomatic of what historian John Higham identifies as the American propensity for ethnic and racial "boundary-building" that flourished during the twenties and thirties. Significantly, the reporters' interest in and intolerance for patterns of ethnic and racial behavior strongly suggest that the social and economic stresses of the Great Depression exacerbated already existing urban racial and ethnic tensions. This presaged on the one hand the racial violence of World War II and, on the other, the trend toward black ghettoization and white suburbanization that characterized the post-war era.

The reporters' ethnocentrism revealed itself in the way they categorized the victims of the depression. Generally they divided the urban relief rolls into two distinct client groups: the worthy, who deserved assistance, and the unworthy, who did not. In 1934 the unemployed white-collar worker, the hapless civil engineer, the jobless salesman and his advertising executive neighbor, the out-of-work store clerk, and waitress, all easily qualified as worthy—that is, they were "jobless through no fault of their own." Vagrants, derelicts, criminals, and the sporadically jobless laborer—the traditionally wretched poor—were labeled "undeserving." But also stigmatized among the latter were the recent black migrants to the city and other "new migrants"—the southern Italians, Greeks, Ukranians, Russian Jews, and Polish-Americans who began crowding America's urban slums in the first decades of the twentieth century. At the very least, Hopkins's correspondents accused these new immigrants of ignorance—an incapacity to cope effectively or efficiently with modern urban civilization. At their worst the reporters branded those whom Jacob Riis had called the "Motley Crowd" as being blatantly inferior, and the corpus of America's incipient "permanent poor."

Some of the reporters displayed an intolerance of the plight of the immigrant poor. Touring Buffalo, Martha Bruere found Italians and Poles "most content with home relief, and making the greatest demands on the [relief] staff—a condition," she added, "which seems to be the same everywhere that I have seen.". . .

Thomas Steep displayed some generosity in his treatment of the ethnic groups who lived in the shadow of the Chicago Commons. "The clients in the neighborhood are largely Italian, Polish and Greek," he wrote, and "are known as an excitable people. For the most part they don't know what the

Depression is all about and think the capitalist class is merely taking a rest, indifferent to what happens to poor people."

But while Steep forgave the poverty of Chicago's ethnics, he, like his colleagues, never extended the same sensitivity to urban blacks. In city after city he and the other reporters entertained complaints about the size of the black relief population. For example, Philadelphia's black population was 11 percent; yet, blacks comprised 40 percent of the relief rolls. "Only about one-fourth of the entire relief load is white or 'American born,'" wrote Julian Claff from the City of Brotherly Love. In Detroit, where 10 percent of the population was black and blacks made up 25 percent of those on relief, Louisa Wilson uncovered "a certain amount of 'man-on-the-street' resentment at the high proportion of Negroes on relief." She found the "stigma of relief practically non-existent among Negroes and Negro politicians alert to see that there is no discrimination." Not surprisingly, disdain for blacks on relief bristled most in southern cities such as New Orleans, where caseworkers and supervisors alike concurred that the Negro caseload was much larger than it should be. There was little doubt in Lorena Hickok's mind "that thousands of these Negroes in New Orleans are living much better on relief than they ever did while they were working. You hear the same stories over and over again—Negroes quitting their jobs or refusing to work because they can get on relief." Perhaps only half of these stories were true, she offered, "but that's bad enough." A local relief supervisor believed that the high black caseloads were the result of "the Negro psychology. They are children really. If anything is being given away they want some too." Besides, she told Hickok, "they are accustomed to having things handed out to them by white people.". . .

Work, the Only Answer

What impact did unemployment and relief have on the fabric of American urban life? In pondering the "cross currents of public opinion" encountered in his visits to many western cities, Robert Washburn set forth eloquently and insightfully the crux of the problem facing America in 1934. "Too much of the analysis of opinion abroad and in urban America," he observed, "springs from the forlorn hope of recovery in terms of the prosperity of bygone days. Many [people] continue to look backward to the old order rather than forward to a new order representing adjustment to changed conditions." Consequently, surmised Washburn, "the relief situation is not being intelligently faced. All too many persons focus attention upon the possible abuses of relief and forget the major problem at hand."

Steep, Colcord, Wilson, Gellhorn, and Hickok joined Washburn in advising Hopkins about the gravity of the urban social crisis—a crisis, said the reporters, whereby the growing ranks of the "unworthy," usually unemployable poor contentedly accepted relief while the salvageable poor, those with enough wits and skill left to work—if work could be found—"bitterly chafe under it, ready to revolt if they [see] anything to be gained that way. [Others are] just sinking into apathy, which is perhaps worse." "As for the future, any effective relief policy," Colcord reflected, "must be self-liquidating lest a too liberal relief program would be likely to build up this minority into a permanent relief class." Choosing to slice through the gloom of the depression and end her report on a more optimistic note, Louisa Wilson tossed Hopkins first a bouquet, then a last note of warning: "Your best publicity," she wrote, "has been yourself; most people, unemployed and employed, agree with you that work is the only answer. Anything else is just peanuts, and their ropes are getting thinner and thinner."

Rural Poverty, Drought, and Migration

T.H. Watkins

One of the great tragedies of the depression was that the debilitating economic crisis was accompanied by and considerably worsened by the onset of a severe drought in the American Midwest. The combination of poverty and agricultural devastation ruined hundreds of thousands of farmers and set in motion large-scale migrations of desperate families. Noted historian, biographer, and editor T.H. Watkins here examines the drought and resultant "Dust Bowl," the effects on farmers, and the displaced people, including the "Okies" and others who struck out for California searching for better lives.

For a quarter of a century, Caroline Boa Henderson and her husband Wilhelmine had raised a family and lived out the hardships and rewards of family farming on a homestead near Shelton, Oklahoma. "We have rooted deeply," she wrote in the summer of 1935. "Each little tree or shrub that we have planted, each effort to make our home more convenient or attractive has seemed to strengthen the hope that our first home might also be our last." But now: "[Our] daily physical torture, confusion of mind, gradual wearing down of courage, seem to make that long continued hope look like a vanishing dream."

In 1930, hail had destroyed their wheat crop. In 1931, terrible prices had undercut a reasonably successful crop. They could endure such drawbacks, as they had before. But then came drought, the worst drought in anyone's memory, day after day, week after week, month after month, year after

Excerpted from *The Great Depression*, by T.H. Watkins. Copyright ©1993 by Blackside Inc. Reprinted by permission of Little, Brown and Company.

year of little or no rain, until by 1935 they were facing ruin in a world ruled by the mocking oppression of dust. "There are days," she wrote,

> when for hours at a time we cannot see the windmill fifty feet from the kitchen door. There are days when for briefer periods one cannot distinguish the windows from the solid wall because of the solid blackness of the raging storm. Only in some Inferno-like dream could anyone visualize the terrifying lurid red light overspreading the sky when portions of Texas "are on the air."

The impact of this relentless siege of disaster cannot easily be exaggerated. Agriculture not only was the linchpin of the American economy in the monetary value of what it grew and nurtured—$9.5 billion even in the drought year of 1934—it produced the very stuff of life on which the rest of the nation's industry, society, and culture fed, physically and even psychologically. In 1934, nearly 30 percent of all Americans still lived on farms, and a good part of how the nation viewed itself was rooted in its agricultural traditions and experience. Henry Ford, for one—a titan of modern industry if ever there was one—was so obsessed by his own and the country's rural origins that he spent much of his adult life collecting old houses, barns, farm implements, buggies, and other rural paraphernalia from the countryside, moving them to Michigan, and assembling them in a kind of living museum he called Greenfield Village, outside Dearborn. "The land supports life," he once wrote. "Industry helps man to make the land support him. When industry ceases to do that and supplants the land, and the land is forgotten and man turns to the machine for sustenance, we find that we do not live off the work of our hands but off the fruits of the land."

Choking Clouds of Dust

Now, both the image and the reality of the land were under assault. Natural cycles had combined with human miscalculation to produce the most devastating agricultural disaster in American history—and little the New Dealers could produce in the way of legislation or emergency measures would do more than provide intermittent and inadequate relief. Drought was nothing new, in this country or any other, but that of the 1930s, which continued through most of the decade—combining in some years with unprecedented heat waves—was "the worst in the climatological history of the country," according to a Weather Bureau scientist. It struck first in the eastern third of the country in 1930, where it crippled agriculture from Maine to Arkansas and where only Florida enjoyed anything that approached normal rainfall. . . .

In 1932, the center of the drought started heading west, and by 1934 it had desiccated the Great Plains from North Dakota to Texas, from the Mississippi River Valley to the Rockies. In the northern Rockies in the winter of 1933–34, the snowpack was less than a third of normal, in the central Rockies less than half, and in areas of the southern Rockies barely a dusting of snow had been seen.

Providence, fate, or some other cosmic force might be blamed for the drought itself, but not for the phenomenon that accompanied it over hundreds of millions of acres: most of that was inescapably man-made. The speculative dance of the war years and the twenties had abused millions of acres of farmland in the South and Midwest, as farmers plowed, planted, and harvested as much as they could as often as they could. Much of the topsoil was left so exhausted it could barely support the most undemanding ground cover, much less productive crops. Careless plowing had rutted the fields, leaving the land open to gullying from erosion. "Since the cover was first disturbed [in the nineteenth century]," a state commission of the National Resources Planning Board reported, "Iowa has lost approximately 550,000 tons of good surface soil per square mile, or a total of thirty billion tons." Iowa was not alone. "Approximately 35 million acres of formerly cultivated land have essentially been destroyed for crop production," the 1934 *Yearbook of Agriculture* reported, adding that "100 million acres now in crops have lost all or most of the topsoil; 125 million acres of land now in crops are rapidly losing topsoil. . . ." At the same time, decades of overgrazing by cattle and sheep ranchers in the western plains and valleys had left one former rich grassland after another stripped clean of ground cover, vulnerable to rampant wind and water erosion. Grass, a Texas sheepherder of the time commented, "is what counts. It's what saves us all—far as we get saved. Men and towns and such as that, don't amount to a particular damn anyhow. Grass does. Grass is what holds the earth together." Not everyone had understood that simple fact. Since the first great cattle and sheep herds had been turned out in the last third of the nineteenth century to feed on the rich grasslands of the plains and mountain pastures of the interior West, the grass had been steadily, ruthlessly overgrazed, until the earth over enormous stretches of land was no longer held together by anything but inertia. After the wartime and postwar booms of the teen years and the 1920s, more than half the grazing land in the western states was in a condition of soil depletion described by the Department of Agriculture as "extreme" or "severe."

The soil, loose and dry, lay unprotected from the winds, which repeatedly swept down on the ruined grasslands of the west, scooped them clean and carried the dust into the air, moving east to the exposed and waiting farmlands of the plains. Here, the winds deposited much of it, moved it around, added to it, filled the air now with the western grasslands dust and the plains farmland dust in a great choking geographic mix. . . . The dust did not always stay west of the Mississippi. When conditions were right, the wind would carry it east on the jet stream in enormous clouds and drop it in the form of filthy unseasonal snow on Chicago, Indianapolis, Washington, New York, and even on the gently rolling decks of Atlantic liners. During just one storm between May 9 and May 11, 1934, an estimated 350 million tons of soil disappeared from the West and reappeared in the East. Chicago got four pounds of it for every person in the city, and Washington, New York, Boston and other cities burned their streetlamps in the middle of the day. . . .

The Dynamics of Dispossession

Many people simply pulled up stakes and abandoned their land, and even for many of those who might have stuck it out in spite of all that nature could do, financial circumstances would make it all but impossible. Resident and absentee owners alike lost their lands to foreclosure proceedings; according to Department of Agriculture reports, nearly two hundred out of every thousand farms in the states of the Midwest, the Central South, and the Plains succumbed to forced sales between 1930 and 1935. And when landlords failed, so did croppers and tenant farmers, and to the ranks of dispossessed owners were added thousands of men and women who were forced off land they had worked as if it were their own. . . .

The opportunities for various forms of theft were irresistible to many owners, who persuaded their croppers and tenant farmers to sign away their shares by threats or subterfuge, or underpaid them, or simply kept the government's payments for themselves without bothering to resort to any special tactics. On one typical plantation, a later government report would say, the owner's gross income had increased from $51,554 in 1932 to $102,202 in 1934, while that of his sharecroppers and tenant farmers had fallen from $379 to $355.

Further, with cotton acreage reduced from 35 million acres in 1932 to 26.5 in 1934–35, the labor force required to plow, plant, and pick the crop was sharply reduced, particularly in those instances when acreage reduction was combined with a rise in the use of tractors and other mechanized equipment. As a consequence, thousands of sharecropper and tenant families found themselves forced off the land— "displaced," as the federalese of the time put it. "I let 'em all go," one Oklahoma landlord frankly admitted.

> In '34 I had I reckon four renters and I didn't make anything. I bought tractors on the money the government give me and got shet o' my renters. You'll find it everywhere all over the country that way. I did everything the government said—except keep my renters. The renters have been having it this way ever since the government come in.

No one knows precisely how many families were displaced in the early years of the New Deal—or just how many had left the land as the direct result of crop reductions or tractor use. However many, there was not much in the way of employment the affected states could offer these suddenly landless and workless thousands; in Arkansas, for example, the unemployment rate was 39 percent in 1933, and in Missouri, Oklahoma, and Texas it ranged from 29 to 32 percent. People began to leave their home states in growing numbers after the terrible summer of 1934. Oklahoma had a net loss of more than 440,000 people in the 1930s. Kansas lost 227,000. Throughout the Plains states, 2.5 million people ultimately would leave for other parts. Most of those parts were nearby; the greater portion of the internal population movement in the American middle in those years was from one state to a neighboring state. But some 460,000 people moved to the Pacific Northwest, where they found work on the building of Bonneville and Grand Coulee dams, found abandoned homesteads they could work in southern Idaho and the eastern valleys of Oregon and Washington, went into the ancient forests of the region as lumberjacks or joined the migrant workers in the hop fields and beet fields—or simply settled in the cities and collected relief checks where and when they could.

A Paradise to Live in or See

Other thousands, particularly from the southwestern Plains states, headed for California. All logic dictated the move, so it seemed. After all, between 1910 and 1930 an estimated 310,000 southwesterners had already moved to the Golden State, lured by the promise of opportunity that had bathed California in the glow of hope ever since the Gold Rush of 1848–52. Residents of Oklahoma, Arkansas, Texas, and other states who had fallen upon hard times now thought of all the cheerful letters they had been receiving from friends and relatives in California, took a look at the tormented land and overburdened cities of their own regions, and put together the wherewithal to get themselves and their families across the plains and deserts to the golden valleys of the West Coast. In one fifteen-month period alone, some 86,000 did precisely that, individually and as families, by car and by bus, most of them taking no more than three or four days to rattle down Route 66 to the border crossing at Yuma, Arizona. By the end of the decade another 220,000 or so would do the same. If many of these people were hard-pressed by farm failure or urban unemployment, most were less than destitute or without family support. They had relatives waiting to house and feed them, if nothing else, and some even had jobs waiting for them. That still left tens of thousands who legitimately could be described as rural refugees, and one thing they soon learned was that land monopoly and agriculture on an industrial scale was a California tradition and the opportunities to engage in family farming were limited to the point of nonexistence. More than 100,000 of the migrants consequently did not gravitate toward the state's farming regions, but to the city of Los Angeles, with some going down to San Diego or up to San Francisco.

Authorities in Los Angeles were less than pleased. The city's relief program was among the best in the country, but it was stretched to its limits and the last thing the city needed—or at least wanted—was another influx of potential welfare recipients, particularly when it was having at least some success in moving trainloads of Mexican-American *repatriados* out of town. . . .

Most of California's new population would become irretrievably urban, whether it had started out that way or not, scattering through poor and middle-class white Los Angeles neighborhoods and out into the bungalow-and-apartment-building suburbs of Long Beach, Compton, Encino, Gardena, Covina, Southgate, Downey, and other towns. But some of those with rural roots would seek the work that was most familiar to them, joining California's drifting population of about 200,000 migrant farm laborers—the largest regional segment of the great army of migrant farm laborers in the United States, a constantly moving and nearly invisible population of as many as two million men, women, and children who cut cane in Florida and dug potatoes in Maine, picked peaches in Georgia and apples in Pennsylvania, plucked strawberries in Louisiana and dug sugar beets in

Michigan, and harvested wheat from central Texas to northern Montana.

Some 110,000 people from the new migration would move to agricultural areas of California—more than seventy thousand of them to the San Joaquin Valley alone. Not all these new arrivals would become migrant laborers, of course, but most did, taking their place in the cheap labor pool that California's agricultural industry had come to expect as its due; for more than eighty years, it had capitalized upon successive waves of Chinese, white native Americans from earlier periods of economic stress, Japanese, Indian (from India), Filipino, and, most recently, Mexican-American laborers. . . .

"Okies" and "Arkies"

Before long, this latest resource of cheap labor would account for nearly half the total of all the state's migrant workers. Like their predecessors, most Anglo migrants confined themselves to journeys up and down the state, following the cycles of planting and harvest from the Imperial Valley to the Sacramento Valley and all the valleys in between, though some backtracked to the cotton fields and other irrigated crops of Arizona or continued straight up California to Oregon and Washington to work the hop fields and beet fields of the north. The average distance traveled from crop to crop every year, the State Relief Administration calculated, was 516 miles. The migrants frequently traveled and worked as families, living in the squalor of work camps either erected by themselves wherever they could with whatever they could or provided by the farmers. Whether self-built or furnished, these feculent little communities, often called "ditch camps" because they were located on the side of roads along which ran filthy water ditches, were disease-ridden and indisputably unfit for human beings. At one point . . . fifty babies died of diarrhea and enteritis in one county during just one picking season; children in Tulare County were reported dying at the rate of two a day; and during an inspection tour of eighteen camps in the vicinity of Kingsburg in Kings County, one social worker found "dozens of children with horribly sore eyes; many cases of cramps, diarrhea, and dysentery; fever, colds, and sore throats." Hookworm, pelle-gra, and rickets were common. Pay was better than it was in the depressed regions of the South and the Midwest, but whether by the day or by the amount of fruit picked or vegetables dug, wages were still far below what a family needed for decent upkeep. What was more, the seasonal character of the job made it impossible to accumulate a significant stake even when one or more members of the family made up to $3 a day, as many did. The recorded need for seasonal labor in the California fields over one two-year period, for example, ranged from a low of 48,173 workers in March to a high of 144,720 in September. Average annual farm labor income, as a consequence, never got much above $1,300 for each family—nearly $500 less than other Anglo California families (though $315 more than the average for *non-Anglo* Californians).

Huddling to wait out off-season unemployment in makeshift "shack-towns" and "Little Oklahomas" perched on the outskirts of agricultural service centers like Bakers-field, Fresno, and Modesto, collecting state relief, sending their children to local schools, the migrants soon earned the pious contempt of their neighbors in the traditional manner of humans rejecting outsiders who are unfamiliar and therefore vaguely threatening. Whatever their origin, they became known collectively as "Okies" and "Arkies," with a few "Texies" thrown in for good measure, and were subject to the kind of abuse and discrimination that the state's Mexican-American, Filipino, and African-American field workers had endured as a matter of course for decades. "These 'share croppers,'" one woman complained, "are not a noble people looking for a home and seeking an education for their children. They are unprincipled degen-erates looking for something for nothing." Interviewing customers at several Sacramento Valley bars, a reporter collected a good run of comments: "Damned Okies." "No damned good. Don't do a damned thing for the town." "Damned shiftless nogoods." "Damned Okies. Damned bums clutter up the roadside."

They possessed a terrible patience, however, these despised migrants, as well as a burning determination and an anger to which someone would be forced to answer sooner or later. But it would be another season or two before the New Dealers would comprehend the full dimensions of what had fallen on these wanderers and begin, slowly and indecisively, to give them sanctuary.

The Struggles of American Blacks

Edwin P. Hoyt

When the Great Depression struck the United States in the 1930s, black Americans had two strikes against them— extreme financial difficulties, which most whites had to deal with too, and also racial bigotry, which ensured that blacks usually did not receive their fair share of government relief. In this excerpt from his insightful study of the depression—*The Tempering Years*—distinguished journalist and scholar Edwin P. Hoyt describes the hardships and often unequal and unjust treatment endured by blacks in these years. Hoyt effectively highlights the discussion with references to the early life and career of famed boxer Joe Louis, whose struggles symbolized those of other American blacks.

The plight of the Negro in America was always the special concern of white men and women of liberal thought. Liberal whites brought the Negro out of physical slavery. They cajoled and shouted and wrote stirringly of the brotherhood of man. Yet in the third decade of the twentieth century, sixty years after Abraham Lincoln's Emancipation Proclamation, the Negro in America was still all too much a slave in fact. He had even lost the benefit of the single positive attribute of slavery: the responsibility of the slave holder to look after the welfare of his slaves.

In North and South, American Negroes were mistreated and segregated. Manners were different but results were the same. The Negro quarters of southern cities were slums in which thousands of people mingled in such miserable condi-

Reprinted with the permission of Scribner, a division of Simon & Schuster, from *The Tempering Years*, by Edwin P. Hoyt. Copyright ©1963 by Edwin Palmer Hoyt, Jr.

tions that white Americans in Boston would not believe they existed in the United States. But what of New York's Harlem? That city within a city was a sordid segregated area marked off from the rest of Manhattan as clearly as though the whites had erected a stone wall around a Negro ghetto.

The whites had produced a few national leaders who tried to better the lot of colored Americans but in the twentieth century the Negro's affairs became the special province of the radical political movements in America. Eugene Debs, then Norman Thomas, the leaders of the Socialist party, strained to organize Negro labor in the South, and so did the American branch of the international Communist movement after 1921. . . .

Traditionally, the Negro was Republican, for the Republicans had freed him from slavery of one kind. But Negro political affiliation was nominal at best. Actually, a handful of Negro politicians had no trouble delivering votes to both parties because the Negro in Harlem or the Negro in southern states where the colored man was allowed to vote was too downtrodden and too uninterested to worry about theoretical freedom.

Negroes secured a special justice in America—harsher than the justice meted out to whites. They performed the same work alongside white workers, and received less pay for it. They were the last hired and the first fired. Few Negroes took any interest in education or self-improvement because they had learned from painful experience that no matter how much they exercised their brains, there was a low ceiling on accomplishment for Negroes in the white community, and there was no mixed community. Not since the days of reconstruction had there been Negroes in Congress. The Negro who attained a federal job or a clerkship with any arm of government was notable enough to be mentioned prominently in the Negro press. . . .

Growing Up in the American South

In the depression of the 1930's Negroes suffered more than any other group in North or South, even more than any other minority. The Chinese and other small non-white communities had a history of taking care of their own people. But there were twelve million Negroes in the United States, more Negroes in America than there were Greeks in Greece.

Nor was there enough Negro money. Negroes had always faced great difficulty in establishing business enterprises. White bankers usually refused to loan money on Negro property.

The eminent Negro successes occurred in the insurance business (insuring Negroes), in the cosmetics business (cosmetics for Negroes), in the professions (serving Negroes), in Negro banking, and in the underworld. Even in the underworld, however, the Negro was segregated.

World War I had caused thousands of Negroes to move north from cotton fields to work in factories. One youth who came this route was to become the most important symbol of the American Negroes since Booker T. Washington and a great asset to all Americans. His name was Joseph Louis Barrow. His great-great-grandfather was a slave named Anthony. His great-great-great-grandfather was a white Alabama planter. Joseph Louis Barrow's grandmother was descended from a Cherokee Indian and from a half-breed Negro slave overseer.

This boy's early life was spent in the Negro poverty of the Deep South. He was born on May 13, 1914, just before World War I began. His father, Mun Barrow, was a share-cropping cotton planter who worked a farm outside the little town of Lafayette, Alabama. The farm was not much. It consisted of 120 acres, located on the edge of the foothills of the Buckalow mountains, but who was to measure? The soil was not productive. Mun Barrow never did own the farm, of course. He lived out his life as a tenant farmer, who shared his crop with the owner, and then was cheated by the local white storekeeper who carried him on credit between crops. Cotton share-cropping was viable enough during the First World War, when the American government and its allies bought all the cotton that could be produced on any land. Five years after the boy's birth, however, the bottom fell out of the cotton market. There were eight children then.

The strain, the debt, the worries of life sapped Mun Barrow's strength. Eventually his mind, not his body, fell sick, and he was committed to a state institution. The mother of Joseph Louis stayed on in the house with the children, and the children sporadically attended a one-room school nearby. The school was colored and segregated, of course, but Joseph Louis and the others who were old enough for school learned the rudiments of reading and writing and arithmetic there.

A few years after Mun Barrow's commitment, his wife went to live with another sharecropper named Patrick Brooks. It was not long before Patrick Brooks discovered that it was impossible to feed and clothe so many bodies with the money to be earned in a depressed farm area. Like thousands of other Negroes, Patrick Brooks heard of the jobs to be found in the North. The family pulled up the shallow roots grown in six generations in Alabama and moved to Detroit without a qualm, so little was there in their native land to hold them there. Save for memories of a handful of Negro neighbors there remained in Alabama no trace of the Mun Barrow family after Mun Barrow himself died in the institution a few years later.

Life for a Young Black in Detroit

Joseph Louis Barrow was in his early teens when the family moved into a crowded tenement on Madison Avenue in the colored district of Detroit. His education had been so neglected that he was enrolled in the third grade. The boy was not brilliant but he completed that grade, and shortly afterward was transferred, to Detroit's Bronson Trade School to learn cabinetmaking.

Joseph Louis Barrow's first job in Detroit was on an ice wagon. He received a dollar a week and tips for lugging twenty-five and fifty-pound cakes of ice up the stairs of the tenements. Joseph Louis Barrow developed huge arm and shoulder muscles, which were later to play an important part in his career.

For a time Joseph Louis worked on a street crew, and for a time after he left the trade school, he worked for the Briggs motor manufacturing company as a laborer, at twenty-five dollars a week.

Before Joseph Louis left school, he had learned something about boxing. Until he began fighting, first for glory, Joseph Louis had been a shy, retiring boy. He did not belong to any street-gang, although they were common then in De-

---

Perpetuating the Unequal Status Quo

This is an excerpt from an October 1934 article by University of North Carolina sociologist Guy Johnson, who points out the racial obstacles then faced by American blacks, even in the initial New Deal programs designed to alleviate the economic crisis.

Even in the administration of federal relief, . . . there has been, particularly in the lower South, a tendency to perpetuate the existing inequalities. Negro tenants received pitifully little of the crop reduction money last fall. Landlords quite generally took charge of the checks and applied them to back debts of the tenants. Furthermore, many landlords are known to have "understandings" with local relief administrators to prevent the "demoralization" of their Negro labor, and it is reported that some go as far as to charge to their tenants' accounts all food and other supplies furnished by the relief office. The director of relief in a southern seaboard city remarked not long ago, "I don't like this fixing of a wage scale for work relief. Why, the niggers in this town are getting so spoiled working on these relief jobs at thirty cents an hour that they won't work on the docks for fifty cents a day like they did last year." In allotting C.W.A. [Civil Works Administration] jobs, reemployment offices throughout the South ignored the Negro skilled worker almost as effectively as if he did not exist. In one tobacco center, for example, 13 per cent of the white C.W.A. workers received the skilled rates of pay, while only 1.2 per cent of the Negro workers received such pay. In another industrial city, 15 per cent of the whites on C.W.A. pay rolls received skilled rates, but not one Negro did so. If skilled Negroes worked, they worked at the unskilled rates.

Quoted in William Dudley, ed., *The Great Depression: Opposing Viewpoints.* San Diego: Greenhaven Press, 1994, p. 185.

troit. He spent his free time sleeping or listening to the radio. He attended the Baptist church with his mother and his brothers and sisters. His one vice was an inordinate appetite for fried chicken.

Fighting was Joseph's principal diversion. It cost nothing to go to Brewster's East Side Gymnasium. There he joined a boxing club and began to train for amateur tournaments.

These 1930's were difficult years for the wife and children of Mun Barrow. Joseph Louis's mother was forced to accept public assistance. She received a little more than thirty dollars a month during that one cheerless winter to help her feed her large family.

But in this period of depression Detroit was not the only city in which people suffered, or even where the Negroes suffered more, proportionally, than the whites. The Negroes always suffered more.

In the summer of 1932 conditions had grown so serious for Negroes in Washington, D.C. that 7,200 Negroes lined up to apply for assistance in the newly opened Emergency Relief Bureau—Herbert Hoover's answer to unemployment. Those Negroes represented 80 per cent of the total applicants for relief.

Shortly before the 1932 Presidential election, a survey by the Baltimore *Afro-American* showed that across the country the Negro population was dependent more on relief in proportion to numbers than any other group of Americans. Few Negroes had savings, because American Negroes had no opportunity to earn enough money to put aside savings.

Negroes had built thirty successful insurance companies in the nation before the crash. After 1929 the number began to dwindle, as families dropped programs or cut their insurance. All Negro business suffered disproportionately except that of the Negro loan-sharks and the racketeers, who preyed on American Negro society in the cities just as other racketeers preyed on the whites.

The Black Vote

Nevertheless, when the nation went to the polls in 1932, the Negro vote was delivered, as was traditional, to the Republican party. Except for a handful of malcontents, the Negroes had never seriously considered switching to the Democratic party.

Once the election was over, the Negroes took a second look at Franklin Delano Roosevelt. In the campaign the new President had promised the Negroes of America that they would become first-class citizens if he was elected. His promises had not won him many votes in Harlem, Detroit, or other Negro voting strongholds, but he was nonetheless to be held to account for his views.

Less than a week after the Presidential election the Pittsburgh *Courier* listed its demands on the administration in behalf of American Negroes. Mr. Roosevelt must:

1. End discrimination in Civil Service.
2. End segregation of Negroes in government departments.
3. End Jim Crow in interstate travel.
4. Urge Congress to enforce the 14th and 15th Amendments to the Constitution.
5. Increase the number of Negroes in government jobs.
6. Follow a hands-off policy toward Haiti and Liberia.
7. Recognize the special problems of Negroes and improve their status.
8. Put an end to the breakup of Negro regiments in the army and open the technical branches of the army and the navy to Negroes.

Negroes had heard promises about equality before. They were not quick to leap to the praise of Franklin Roosevelt, no matter what he promised. They would wait and see.

The Negroes of America did not have to wait too long before there were matters of interest for them to consider in the actions of the federal government.

One of Franklin Delano Roosevelt's first Presidential acts indicated that the role of the Negro in American society was going to change during his administration. In March, 1933, when Roosevelt held his first press conference, Edgar G. Brown, the correspondent of the Chicago *Defender*, stood in the room with other American newspaper correspondents and listened to the new President. Brown was the first Negro newspaperman ever to be admitted to a White House conference. . . .

A Friend in the White House?

There was no quick victory—as the watchers suspected. Industry continued to discriminate against Negroes, in North and South. But in 1933 and 1934 Franklin Roosevelt continued to show sympathy for Negro Americans and concern about their problems.

By the middle of 1934 the Negroes were beginning to accept the idea that they might, for the first time in seventy years, truly have a friend in the White House. Harry Hopkins appointed Negro assistants to administer his relief program. Harold Ickes, once head of the Chicago chapter of the NAACP, appointed Negroes to help him. Walter White was asked to serve on the Virgin Islands advisory board. Another Negro, Henry A. Hunt, of Fort Valley, Virginia, was appointed to administer the farm credit program among Negroes. It was a novelty for a Negro to achieve such high office.

In 1934, the national average of Americans on relief was fixed at around 10 per cent. With Negroes, the figure was far higher. In New York 25 per cent of the Negro population was on the dole. In Florida 36 per cent of Negroes were receiving relief. In some states of the Deep South the number of Negroes was smaller, because the Negroes were refused relief and told by local authorities to "go pick cotton" when they asked for aid. Discrimination in the NRA wage rates continued. Discrimination in AF of L unions continued, too. Negroes were allowed to join the unions but they were not accorded full privileges of membership, and were segregated in local unions or in special units of locals.

Still the Roosevelt administration was finding favor among the Negro people.

Harold Ickes, the Secretary of the Interior, quickly proved himself as good a friend of the Negro as Harry Hopkins was. In October, 1934, Ickes established a subsistence plan, in collaboration with Hopkins. The plan meant a great deal to the poor farmers of the South, Negroes and whites. Three special settlements were established in Alabama. In one type of settlement the farmers were given the use of sixty acres of land, equipment, and training. They were expected to farm full time and to grow cotton, fruit, and dairy products.

A second type of subsistence homestead involved purchase of land farmed by a tenant. The land was then given to the tenant. He was expected to switch from cotton farming to producing dairy products and truck-garden crops.

The third type of homestead was a part-time farm given to an industrial worker who lived on the outskirts of one of the cities. Each of these was a farm of from one to five acres of land. In theory, the worker would earn his basic income from local industry, but would supplement that income with a real income earned from farming. . . .

Franklin Roosevelt had won over many Negroes with a single one of the impulsive, humane gestures of which he was capable. One day in the spring of 1934, Sylvester Harris, a Negro farmer in Columbus, Mississippi, spent his last ten dollars to call Roosevelt and tell him of his desperate circumstances. The President took the call, and heard the farmer's story. When he put down the telephone, the President ordered that something be done for Harris and for all the farmers in that condition. A week later Harris had been granted a federal loan (which he repaid in time), and a few months later, the nation had been given the subsistence plan. The dividends Roosevelt collected included Harris's support of the Democrats during the 1934 Congressional elections, a Thanksgiving turkey from the Harris farm, and the gratitude of thousands of poor farmers.

Joe Louis's Struggle

Joseph Louis Barrow had been making something of himself in one of the few ways open to a young Negro. Joseph applied himself to boxing and became so adept that by 1933 he was sent to Boston to fight for the light-heavyweight title in the National AAU championships. Joseph lost the title to Max Marek, a Notre Dame football player, but in the ring, at least, Joseph Louis Barrow was on even terms with the white man. Here was one of the areas of life in which a poor, uneducated boy could hope to rise to fame and fortune.

In the year of the AAU championship fight, Joseph Louis Barrow was taken under the promotional wing of John Roxborough, one of the most prominent members of Detroit Negro society. Roxborough was ostensibly engaged in the insurance business. He was a college man, from the University of Michigan. He also had a police record and was suspected of participation in the rackets of Detroit. By Negro standards, however, John Roxborough was considered an honest and admirable man. The Negroes, pressed so far down by the whites, given harsh tastes of white man's justice, possessed a different standard of morality than the whites. To them the underworld was real and understandable. There was no conflict, to Negroes, in a John Roxborough with a police record who asked this new young fighter to promise that he would never do a single thing that would bring discredit on the Negro race.

Having made those statements, Roxborough then sought the participation of Julian Black, a Negro real estate man in Chicago to help share expenses of training the new fighter. He also changed the name of the fighter to Joe Louis.

John Roxborough had no difficulty in persuading Joe Louis to behave. Joe was not an intellectual but he was aware of the problems of the Negro in American society. If he could make the top rung of the boxing ladder, he vowed that he would become "a credit to the race."

In 1934 Joe won the light-heavyweight amateur title in a fight at St. Louis and made the decision to turn professional. Jack Blackburn, a wily old Negro fighter-turned-manager, was persuaded to train the young, raw recruit. Blackburn shook his head at first. He did not want to be associated with a Negro fighter. There was no future in the ring for a Negro as far as he could see. After a few fights had established a reputation, if the Negro fighter would not lie down on cue, the promoters made sure that he got no more bouts. If the fighter followed these rules, after a few years he was a stumblebum or a cripple.

All that argument came before Jack Blackburn saw Joe Louis fight and saw for himself the speed and power in those brawny iceman's shoulders and those heavy laborer's hands.

Blackburn changed his mind. He agreed to train Joe Louis. . . .

Louis had won fifty-four of his fifty-eight amateur fights, and forty-three of them by knockout. But amateur boxing and professional fighting were two different games, and Joe Louis still had much to learn to be a true professional.

The best way to learn was to start fighting. In June, 1934, Louis defeated Jack Krachen in Joe's first professional fight. He earned about fifty dollars. In his fifth fight he knocked out Buck Everett, a professional who had fought some fifty times, and won $250 for that fight.

In December, 1934, sports writers rated Joe a "comer" when he was matched with Lee Ramage, a fighter of some reputation, in a bout at the Chicago Stadium. Joe Louis won by a technical knockout. This was his first taste of bigger money; the Louis crowd received $2,750 as its share, and, more important, the fight established Joe as a drawing card. He was in the big money class at last. . . .

A Symbol of Black Opportunity

As time went on . . . Joe became used to his special position as a symbol of the best of what he called "his race." He continued to live the clean life. When he visited night clubs (which he enjoyed) he ordered drinks for the crowd, but Joe Louis's drink was milk. He kept regular hours, he watched his weight, a difficult task for a man who liked fried chicken. By the end of 1935 Joe Louis had made an amazing monetary record: in one year he had risen from virtual anonymity to fame, and he had earned more than $300,000.

Wealth affected Joe Louis in a simple way that white Americans could understand and laugh about with respect, without bitterness. He bought a house for his mother. He bought a fast car for himself, although he drove too fast and not well enough to please his friends and managers. He bought three dozen new suits, most of them light-colored, and an endless supply of shirts, socks, neckties, and other haberdashery. But his brothers wore his suits and his family and friends spent his money.

Joe was generous. One of his favorite ways of celebrating a victory was to take a half-dozen Detroit neighborhood colored boys to the movies, and afterward to treat them at the local ice-cream parlor. His older friends borrowed money from him and persuaded him to engage in business enterprises which collapsed, one after another.

As time went on Louis was exploited shamelessly by most of those around him, but this did not create feelings of contempt for the young Negro boxer. White boys and colored boys alike could look to him with pride for there were no overtones of racism in him, and he aroused none except in the hearts of the truly vicious. Perhaps one of the secrets of the success of Joe Louis in raising the status of the Negro in America was his own humble attitude.

To some white Americans Louis was a "tough nigger who knew his place," and did not push himself in white society. To others he was a stupid Negro who was born with the animal strength to hit hard with his fists. But to millions, Joe Louis was a great fighter, and because he was so great a fighter, when he fought most Americans forgot for a few moments that he was also a Negro. . . .

The ascendant years of Joe Louis were good years for the Negroes, not solely because of him, and perhaps hardly at all because of his influence except emotionally. Yet Louis was a symbol of opportunity—the sharecropper boy grown successful; and other Negroes looked on him with pride. They also looked upon their government and the Roosevelt administration with increasing favor as their position in America improved. . . .

By 1936 the Negroes had been convinced that the Roosevelt administration was actually dispensing relief and government jobs to them on the same terms as to the whites. Roosevelt had received Negro delegations, including a delegation of Negro Elks. When Mrs. Roosevelt visited Howard University she was photographed with a pair of young Negro ROTC cadets wearing snappy army officers' uniforms. Roosevelt, the Negro press reported, had given more jobs to Negroes than the three previous Republican Presidents combined. Roosevelt denounced lynching, and earned the praise of the Chicago *Defender:* "His New Deal has now become a human deal in which all parts of the nation can feel themselves a part." And Negro intellectuals saw the Roosevelt administration as the fourth major change in America, from their point of view: first was the American Revolution; second was the Jackson election and Jackson's extension of freedom to the common white man; third was the Civil War, which freed the slaves; then came Mr. Roosevelt's Revolution. Joe Louis, even though he did not recognize it himself, was a part of that revolution. The Negroes were beginning to stir, getting ready to demand rights as full-fledged Americans.

Depression-Era Cinema Reflected Social Values

Robert S. McElvaine

American movies were more than mere escapism in the 1930s, Millsaps College scholar Robert S. McElvaine states here. Many of the characters and stories presented in the cinema, he says, affected or reinforced viewers' perceptions and beliefs about individual success, the ethics of big business and workplace competition, societal justice and injustice, and other social phenomena. In this view, widely popular movies like *Little Caesar* and *I Am a Fugitive from a Chain Gang* constituted an expression of the gloomy, desperate national mood of the early 1930s.

Although music, radio, books, magazines, comics, sports, and other forms of mass entertainment were all significant in the thirties, nothing else was as central to American popular culture in that decade as motion pictures. There are good reasons for concentrating attention on Hollywood. Movies were *the* preeminent form of popular culture in the 1930s. Almost everyone who could afford to (and millions who could not) went to the cinema frequently throughout the decade. During the depths of the Depression in the early thirties, an average of 60 million to 75 million movie tickets were purchased each week. Although part of this remarkable figure represented repeat customers, the number itself corresponds to more than 60 percent of the entire American population. (This compares to a number of weekly movie admissions by the late 1970s equaling less than 10 percent of the population.) Hollywood made more than 5000 feature

From *The Great Depression: America 1929–1941*, by Robert McElvaine. Copyright ©1984 by Robert McElvaine. Reprinted by permission of Times Books, a division of Random House, Inc.

films during the 1930s. Up to a point, film producers had to reflect changes in popular attitudes. They were guided by the profit motive and so had an incentive to give moviegoers what they wanted to see. Many contemporaries were convinced that film was the most powerful medium of the time. Immediately after the stock market crash, for instance, New York Mayor Jimmy Walker asked movie operators to "show pictures which will reinstate courage and hope in the hearts of the people." If any form of popular culture can shed light on a people's values, surely the Depression-era cinema is the most likely candidate. My perceptions are based on a study of nearly 150 films of the period, including many of the most popular and significant ones.

The most common impression about movies in the Great Depression is that they served as escapism. Depression victims—and those who feared they might soon be such—could pay their dime or quarter and forget the troubles of the real world for a few hours. Of course this is true. It is undeniable that movies provided a temporary escape for millions during the Depression. But they did far more than that. It was, as [noted historian] Arthur Schlesinger, Jr., has rightly said, a time "When the Movies Really Counted," when they were "near the operative center of the nation's consciousness."

In his history of the films of Depression America, *We're in the Money*, Andrew Bergman insists that the movies of the period served to reinforce the success ethic and values of what I have here termed acquisitive individualism. "Dehumanizing competition," Bergman contends, was glorified in most thirties films. The only exception he finds is King Vidor's *Our Daily Bread* (1934). That film glorifies life on a collective farm and favorably portrays the whole idea of cooperative living. Bergman is right in singling out *Our Daily Bread* for its powerful plea for cooperation and even collectivism, but I think he is quite wrong in suggesting that most films made during the Depression carried a message extolling the virtues of competitive individualism. On the contrary, movie audiences were able to take away from many thirties productions reinforcement of the moral economic values that they were developing on their own.

A Love/Hate Attitude Toward Success

The first—and most enduring—of the popular genres of the Depression years, the gangster film, makes the point clearly. These movies have generally been taken to have represented one of several viewpoints. Bergman argues that they provided a vehicle for the traditional American story of individual success. Robert Warshow, on the other hand, in his highly perceptive 1948 essay "The Gangster as Tragic Hero," maintains that the ultimate message of the gangster film is that in modern, individualistic, success-oriented society "there is really only one possibility—failure." The gangster, many critics have pointed out, is a figure with whom audiences identified, particularly in the early Depression years. "[T]he gangster speaks for us," Warshow says, "expressing that part of the American psyche which rejects the qualities and demands of modern life, which rejects 'Americanism' itself."

The criminal must either represent the American success ethic or its rejection. We cannot have it both ways. Or can we? "We gain the double satisfaction," Warshow points out, "of participating vicariously in the gangster's sadism and then seeing it turned against the gangster himself." The gangster "is what we want to be and what we are afraid we may become." This insight provides the key to understanding how the public perceived the gangster movie in the early Depression. Americans have always had a love/hate attitude toward individual success. On the one hand, we have a burning desire to succeed; on the other, we despise the successful man who steps on others to get ahead. This amounts to a different way of stating the conflict between the competing American value systems: acquisitive individualism *versus* cooperative or ethical individualism. In a period like the 1920s, the worship of success takes precedence; but in the Depression many Americans concluded, as Warshow put it, "the successful man is an outlaw."

Equating Crime with Business

The prototype of the early thirties gangster genre—and its most important example—was *Little Caesar* (1930). Contrary to the popular assumption that the gangster is a film character with which the audience identifies, the central character of this film, Caesar "Rico" Bandello (Edward G. Robinson), is anything but sympathetic. His goals are to make money and, even more, to "be somebody," to be in a position to tell others what to do. Rico destroys anything and anyone who stands in the way of his advancement. He is the epitome of the self-centered, acquisitive man, one who will use any means of "competition" to eliminate (often literally) his rivals. In short, Little Caesar stood in the eyes of early Depression audiences (the movie was released in January 1931) as the symbol of the amoral, greedy businessman. For those who may have missed the connection, Rico makes it explicit as he arrives in the upper reaches of crime: "Yeah, I ain't doin' so bad in this business, so far," he tells his associate. The equation of crime and business was one that Depression viewers appreciated (so much so that in 1933 critic Dwight MacDonald called Little Caesar "the most successful talkie that has yet been made in this country").

The message Depression-era audiences were likely to carry away from Little Caesar was quite the opposite of reinforcement of the individual success ethic. The film could instead be seen as an implicit condemnation of the amoral marketplace values that dominated the preceding decade. In his drive for the top, Rico has no truck with compassion or human values. "Love, soft stuff!" he says disgustedly to his friend Joe Masara. Rico realizes that the man on the make cannot be soft; he must be able to "dish it out" and "take it." Rico's collapse (like that of American business) is even more rapid than his rise, and begins because of his insistence that Joe must come back to work with him. Although Rico says "this is what I get for liking a guy too much," his real motive was to control Joe and protect himself. Selfishness, not friendship (despite the homosexual undertones in the movie), leads to Rico's demise. As he dies in a shootout—beneath a billboard announcing Joe's success as a performer—Caesar utters his famous last words: "Mother of Mercy, is this the end of Rico?" The obligatory end for the gangster has arrived. The prophecy at the film's outset, where Matthew is quoted ("For those who live by the sword shall also die by the sword"), seems fulfilled. What is often over-looked, however, is that Little Caesar never quite reached the top. One step above him was the head of the city's criminals, appropriately called Big Boy. ("I never saw anybody the Big Boy couldn't get to," says Little Arnie Lorch. "He can fix anything. That's why he's the Big Boy.") The audience—or at least that part of it that noticed—was left with the message that the biggest gangster of them all continues to thrive. The implications for the "big boys" of the economic system in the thirties was apparent.

"I Ain't So Tough"

The same sort of implicit attack on the amoral methods of acquisitive individualism was evident in other films of the early Depression. Chester Morris, the central character in *Corsair* (1931), wants to show his girlfriend that he is "as good a businessman" as her father, who is a stockbroker. To do so, he becomes a pirate! Chester sums up the view of business ethics that was rapidly gaining acceptance in these years: "It doesn't matter how you make your money, it's how much you have when you quit."

But all gangsters in the movies were not alike. If Robinson's Rico was not the sort with whom the viewer was likely to identify, the same could hardly be said of James Cagney as Tommy Powers in *Public Enemy* (1931). Here is the other side of the ambivalence toward the anarchic criminal figure. Viewers could identify with Powers not only because Cagney portrayed a more likable fellow than did Robinson, but because the Cagney character was not entirely self-centered. Powers and another character, Paddy Ryan, are obviously "good" mobsters. "Nobody can do much without somebody else," Ryan says. There is some indication in the movie that Tommy became a criminal because of societal injustice, although this is not explored. In any event, Tom Powers believes in "justice" of a sort—in honor among thieves. He does not go around killing people for fun. (Rico usually had some small reason for his murders, but he obviously enjoyed them.) In the end, Tom is sorry for his life of crime. The sharp contrast with Rico is evident in Powers's dying words: "I ain't so tough." Just so. That is why we like him so much better than Rico. Unlike Little Caesar, Tom Powers is not the completely ruthless reflection of the acquisitive businessman stereotype. The moviegoer was able to take vicarious enjoyment when someone like Powers, with his ultimate sense of justice, "stuck it to" a society that had seemingly become so unjust.

Robin Hoods and Folk Heroes

Gangsterism in the early thirties was not, of course, a phenomenon confined to the silver screen. Popular attitudes toward real criminals paralleled the feelings evoked by movie mobsters. Even if they would not admit it, many people identified up to a point with the real gangsters they read about in the newspapers. It was not, however, brutality and selfishness that the public was approving. The popular mood found it agreeable to romanticize the criminals, to see them as social bandits who robbed bankers and gave to the poor. Seeing Depression criminals as Robin Hoods was best exemplified in Woody Guthrie's 1939 song "The Ballad of Pretty Boy Floyd." Guthrie's mythicized Floyd had been unjustly accused of crime and had gone on to become a folk hero:

> *There's many a starving farmer the same*
> *old story told*
> *How the outlaw paid their mortgage and*
> *saved their little home.*

Guthrie's closing verses made the point that many others left unarticulated in their romanticizing of criminals:

> *Yes, as through this world I ramble,*
> *I see lots of funny men,*
> *Some will rob you with a 6-gun, and*
> *some will rob you with a pen.*
> *But as through your life you'll travel,*
> *wherever you may roam,*
> *You won't never see an outlaw drive*
> *a family from their home.*

In point of fact, few Robin Hoods were roaming the

American countryside in the Depression. Floyd, "Baby Face" Nelson, John Dillinger, Bonnie Parker and Clyde Barrow, and the rest were cold-blooded murderers, largely devoid of the human sympathies some observers like to find in them. It must be realized, though, that people who identified with them were making them over in the social bandit image. Their minds created what they wanted to see and then admired it. The songs about the bandits survived, as Eric Hobsbawm has noted that they traditionally did with social bandits

The Gangsters Understand the System

Noted film historian Jack Ellis here suggests that movie gangsters of the 1930s understood well how to succeed in the era's "corrupt" system.

If the musical sometimes offered masked representations of the Depression society of the thirties, the gangster film seemed to present a metaphorical explanation of what had gone wrong with the country. The goals of the gangster protagonists [leading characters] are confined to acquiring wealth and power. They are the ones who understand the system and how to succeed within it. Others, those who believe in honest work, loyalty, affection, and decency are ineffectual dupes. In those films gangsterism can be seen as super-capitalism. . . . If gangsters are businessmen as well as criminals, might it not be equally true that businessmen are gangsters? Couldn't utilities magnate [mogul] Samuel Insull be seen as a legitimized Al Capone? In any case, the little man was caught in a corrupt system which the greedy and ruthless controlled. How come the banks couldn't pay back their investors, anyway? Exactly why was it that profits made on the stock market suddenly became losses? In a later example of a related sub-genre, *The Asphalt Jungle* (1950), the outwardly respectable lawyer secretly involved in criminal activity remarks to his wife, "Crime, my dear, is merely a left-handed form of human endeavor."

Jack C. Ellis, *A History of Film.* Englewood Cliffs, NJ: Prentice-Hall, 1979, p. 205.

in peasant societies. Those songs allowed people to maintain the myths and "the vision of the just society."

A Symbol of Depression Victims

Movies could also deal with issues similar to the Guthrie version of how Pretty Boy Floyd became an outlaw because he was wrongly accused. *I Am a Fugitive From a Chain Gang* (1932) is one of the most powerful films of the period. The hero of this Mervyn Le Roy movie, James Allen (Paul Muni), returns from the World War determined to find a better life than his old job as a shipping clerk in a shoe factory. He does not want a job like his life in the Army, being under orders, working in routines. Rather, Jim wants "a man's job"—an expression frequently used to convey the idea of self-respect and independence: "I've learned that life is more important than a stupid, insignificant job." Jim takes to the road seeking an engineering position, but is able to find only occasional employment. Finally he becomes desperate and tries to hock his war medal, but finds a case in the pawnshop is already filled with them.

Jim meets Pete, another "bum," who tells him he knows where they can get some free hamburgers. Jim's real troubles begin when Pete unexpectedly pulls a gun on the diner's proprietor and forces Jim to join in a robbery. Showing no concern for the circumstances, a judge sentences Jim to ten years at hard labor. The action takes place in an unspecified southern state (although scarcely anyone has an accent), and Jim finds himself on a chain gang. On the surface, *I Am a Fugitive* is an effective attack on the horrors of chain gangs. On a slightly deeper level, it carried a more important meaning to Depression audiences. The prison becomes an exaggerated vision of society. Innocent people are treated brutally. The regimented life from which Jim wanted to escape in the Army and factory is even worse in prison. "You even have to get their permission before you can sweat," another inmate tells Jim. While those in power are cruel and unreasoning, the victims show concern for each other and cooperate as much as they can. An older man, Bomber, advises Jim on how to escape and gives him $7, which it took him years to accumulate. Sebastian, a black prisoner, helps Jim bend his shackles. Muni himself presents a more sympathetic character than he had a few months earlier in his more noted role as the Capone-like leading man in *Scarface* (1932).

After his escape Jim (now calling himself Allen James) becomes a 1920s success story, rising Alger-style in a Chicago engineering firm. His only mistake is to fall into the clutches of a "loose woman" who finds out about his past and threatens to expose him unless he marries her, which he does. Finally, after he asks for a divorce, she turns him in. Because Allen has become such a pillar of the community, all of Chicago comes to his defense and the governor refuses to allow extradition. Then an official of the southern state arrives and promises Jim a full pardon if he will voluntarily return and serve ninety days of easy time.

The state goes back on its promise and Jim is outraged: "The state's promise didn't mean anything! It was all lies! . . . Their crimes are worse than mine, worse than anybody's here. They're the ones who belong in chains, not me!" Jim finally escapes again. Now he symbolizes all Depression victims, desperately searching for any kind of work, a social outcast. He constantly feels hunted, and when he returns to Chicago to see the woman with whom he had fallen in love earlier, Jim hears a noise and, believing the authorities are after him, takes his leave. As his face fades, the woman asks, "How do you live?" From the dark comes a hoarse whisper: "I steal!" And the movie *ends*. No other thirties movie has an ending so cold and depressing. *I Am a Fugitive* was the perfect expression of the national mood in 1932: despair, suffering, hopelessness. Few movies have ever represented a year so well. Le Roy's film *was* 1932: hopelessness. America had hit bottom.

Chapter 3

Roosevelt Comes to Power

Turning | Points

IN WORLD HISTORY

F.D.R. Takes the Reins of State

Samuel Eliot Morison

In this information-packed essay, Samuel Eliot Morison, one of the twentieth century's premiere historians of U.S. history, chronicles the political rise of Franklin D. Roosevelt, how Roosevelt defeated Herbert Hoover in the 1932 national campaign, the surge of confidence that gripped the country following the new president's stirring inaugural address, and the basic political philosophy behind the New Deal he was about to institute.

The eruption of Franklin D. Roosevelt into the political area in 1928 was a surprise. "F.D.R.," born to a patrician Hudson river family in 1882, graduated from Groton and Harvard (where he was regarded as a playboy) and the Columbia Law School. For a few years he engaged in law and business in New York City with very moderate success; but he made a successful marriage in 1905 with Eleanor Roosevelt, niece of his remote cousin Theodore, whom he greatly admired. The Dutchess County Roosevelts to whom Franklin belonged had been Democrats since Andrew Jackson days; so, as a Democrat, "Frank," as his friends called him, was elected to the New York Senate. Support of Woodrow Wilson in the campaign of 1912 earned him the assistant secretaryship of the navy . . . and that, in turn, led to his vice-presidential nomination on the losing [James W.] Cox ticket in 1920. Next year a sudden and severe attack of polio at his summer home in Campobello, New Brunswick, left him apparently a hopeless invalid; but during the next seven years he fought his way back to health, used his leisure for thought, study, and correspondence, and emerged from forced retirement a changed man. Still charming and jaunty in manner, he was

From *The Oxford History of the American People*, by Samuel Eliot Morison. Copyright ©1965 by Samuel Eliot Morison. Used by permission of Oxford University Press, Inc.

deeply ambitious to do something for his country and lend fresh luster to the Roosevelt name.

New York and Beyond

His political comeback was signaled by nominating Al Smith in the Democratic convention of 1924 with the "happy warrior" speech; and Al later persuaded him to take the Democratic candidacy for governor of New York in 1928. To those who objected that Roosevelt was still a cripple, the Happy Warrior replied, "The Governor of New York State does not have to be an acrobat!" Although Al lost his native state in the presidential election, the magic of the Roosevelt name elected F.D.R. governor; and at Albany he did so well, with the assistance of an able staff of economists and social workers, that in 1930 he was re-elected by a majority of 700,000. That made him a leading contender for his party's presidential nomination.

Herbert Hoover was renominated by the Republicans as the only alternative to admitting failure. For the Democratic nomination, assumed to mean election, there was a free-for-all. Al Smith wanted it again, but the politicians recalled his poor showing in 1928 and divided their efforts between F.D.R. and "Cactus Jack" Garner of Texas, then speaker of the house. Other aspirants were William McAdoo, President Wilson's son-in-law; Newton D. Baker, Wilson's able secretary of war; Owen D. Young, who had helped put the German Republic on its financial feet; Governor Harry F. Byrd of Virginia; even Governor "Alfalfa Bill" Murray of Oklahoma. Joseph P. Kennedy, father of a future President, then a free-lance financier who had got out of the stock market in time, decided that Roosevelt was the man. Kennedy raised money for his campaign and attended the nominating convention. When it looked like a deadlock between Roosevelt and Garner, he talked on the telephone to William Randolph Hearst. . . . As the only California Democrat willing to spend money, Hearst controlled the California delegation. They were pledged to Garner, but Kennedy . . . convinced the multimillionaire publisher that if he did not switch California's vote to Roosevelt, either Baker or Smith, both of whom he hated, would be nominated. Hearst switched; Garner, anxious to avoid a deadlock, released his pledged delegates, and California's 44 votes helped to nominate Roosevelt. Garner accepted the vice-presidential nomination, which was more to his liking since it gave him plenty of time for hunting and shooting in Texas.

The 1932 Election

Roosevelt, who before his nomination had seemed to many people merely "a nice man who very much wanted to be President," electrified the country by a bold, aggressive campaign. Although he now had a wide radio network at his disposal, the candidate, to prove his physical vigor and exert his personal magnetism, embarked upon an old-fashioned stumping tour which took him into almost every state of the Union. He set forth a comprehensive scheme of reform and recovery, embracing the repeal of Prohibition, unemployment relief, lower tariffs, and legislation to save agriculture, rehabilitate the railroads, protect consumers and investors, and slash government expenses; all of it contained in the party platform. The keynote was a "New Deal" to the "forgotten man." For some odd reason this last phrase aroused the fury of conservatives; even Al Smith, when he first heard Roosevelt plead for "the forgotten man at the bottom of the economic pyramid," burst out with, "This is no time for demagogues!"

President Hoover, laboring under the dead weight of the deepening depression, recited his efforts to cope with it, mumbled prophecies to the effect that a Democratic victory would mean that "The grass will grow in the streets of a hundred cities," and reaffirmed his faith in rugged individualism and the American system. "Any change of policies will bring disaster to every fireside in America."

Most of the voters, fearing that the "American system" needed desperate measures to be saved, were ready to take a chance on the New Deal. On election day Roosevelt received almost 22.8 million votes with 57.3 per cent of all cast, and won 472 electors; Hoover polled 15.8 million votes—39.6 per cent, with only 59 votes in the electoral college. It is a tribute to the average American's faith in his country and her institutions that the Socialist and Communist parties, both insisting that capitalism had collapsed, polled fewer than a million votes. And the Democrats elected emphatic majorities to both houses of Congress. There was never a stronger popular mandate in American history for a new program or policy. . . . As [the popular humorist] Will Rogers put it, "The little fellow felt that he never had a chance and he dident till November the Eighth. And did he grab it!"

Hoover's Last Gasp

Unfortunately the so-called "lame duck" Amendment XX to the Constitution, altering the beginning of a new presidential administration from 4 March to 20 January, and the opening of a new Congress to 3 January, was not ratified by the requisite number of states until 6 February 1933. Consequently there was an embarrassing gap between the November election and 4 March, when F.D.R. could take over. Hoover at that time made a sincere but fruitless effort to persuade the President-elect to agree to participate in an international conference to stabilize currency and exchange, and to make a public declaration against inflation, expensive government projects, and unbalancing the budget. In other words, the President-elect should (as Hoover wrote to Senator David A. Reed on 20 February) agree to "the abandonment of 90 per cent of the so-called new deal." Roosevelt refused to commit himself in advance to break his platform. . . . Hoover later declared that "fear" of New Deal radicalism was what caused the governors of twenty-two states to close all banks prior to 4 March. But the banks had been falling right through the depression—almost 5000 of them since 1929; and the threatened failure of many more early in 1933 was simply the built-up result of the economic tailspin.

Before we dismiss Herbert Hoover from his unhappy four years in Washington to his happy thirty-one years of semi-retirement, we should remember that some degree of F.D.R.'s success in dealing with the depression is owed to Hoover's proving that conventional methods had failed. If Al Smith, whose economic presuppositions were the same as

Hoover's, had been elected President in 1928, he probably would have repeated the same mistakes.

Leadership of Frankness and Vigor

When Franklin D. Roosevelt took the oath of office on 4 March 1933, the stock market had already started that upswing from its all-time low which continued to 1938. But the general situation was catastrophic, and the new President made no effort to minimize it. The first paragraph of his inaugural address sounded like a trumpet call:

> First of all, let me assert my firm belief that the only thing we have to fear is fear itself—nameless, unreasoning, unjustified terror which paralyzes needed efforts to convert retreat into advance. In every dark hour of our national life a leadership of frankness and vigor has met with that understanding and support of the people themselves which is essential to victory. I am convinced that you will again give that support to leadership in these critical days.

Then came the adagio:

> Values have shrunk to fantastic levels; taxes have risen; our ability to pay has fallen; government of all kinds is faced by serious curtailment of income; the means of exchange are frozen in the currents of trade; the withered leaves of industrial enterprise lie on every side; farmers find no markets for their produce; the savings of many years in thousands of families are gone. More important, a host of unemployed citizens face the grim problems of existence and an equally great number toil with little return. Only a foolish optimist can deny the dark realities of the moment.

. . . Setting forth a general program which he promised shortly to elaborate in detail, he warned Congress and the country that the emergency called for emergency measures; and that if "the normal balance of executive and legislative authority" prove inadequate "to meet the unprecedented task before us," he would ask Congress for "broad executive power to wage a war against the emergency as great as the power that would be given to me if we were in fact invaded by a foreign foe." He concluded:

> The people of the United States . . . in their need . . . have registered a mandate that they want direct, vigorous leadership. They have asked for discipline and direction under

---

Mrs. Roosevelt Pleads for Poor Mothers

This May 12, 1933, AP news item illustrates how, from the moment that Franklin Roosevelt took office as president, his wife worked tirelessly for the rights and benefits of underprivileged and underrecognized groups and individuals.

Mrs. Franklin D. Roosevelt made a plea for poor mothers today after listening to several doctors describe the attention mothers should have. She spoke at a Mother's Day luncheon of the Maternity Center Association.

"The question is not whether you will support the maternity center," Mrs. Roosevelt told her hearers, who included many society women interested in the work of the institution.

"It seems a foregone conclusion that if we are intelligent people, and I think we are, we shall be interested in the care of our mothers.

"As I have been sitting here I have been wondering if we are going to go a step beyond these obvious things, if we are going to think a little about other problems which touch this subject of the health of mothers and children, and if we are going to think about mothers who cannot have the care that these very learned gentlemen have been telling us is so necessary.

"It isn't a question of supporting a thing which we must do, which we know is necessary, but it is a question of whether we are going to have the grit to go back of this and be willing to give up—some of us a great deal more than we have ever given up before—in order that our mothers may have the proper conditions in which to bring their children into the world, and that the world into which those children come may be worth coming into."

Quoted in Associated Press Writers, *The Great Depression, 1929–1939*. Danbury, CT: Grolier, 1995, p. 81.

leadership. They have made me the present instrument of their wishes. In the spirit of the gift I take it. . . . May God guide me in the days to come. . . .

[The next day, March 5] I asked a New Hampshire countrywoman, in a town which always voted heavily Republican, what they thought of the new President. Here is her answer, which millions all over the land would have endorsed: "We feel that our country has been given back to us.". . .

Winning the People's Loyalty

Franklin D. Roosevelt, who occupied the chief magistracy for twelve years and thirty-nine days, was one of the most remarkable characters who ever occupied that high office; and he held it during two major crises, the Great Depression and World War II. . . . He really loved people as no other President has except Lincoln. . . . Widely traveled in youth and young manhood, Roosevelt knew Europe well. A great reader, especially of American history and political science, he found time to collect postage stamps and books on the United States Navy. . . . In addition, he had political acumen, a sense of the "art of the possible," and knew how to work through established political machinery. . . . He summoned all manner of experts to Washington to furnish ideas and formulate legislation to get the country out of its desperate plight. He combined audacity with caution; stubborn as to ultimate ends, he was an opportunist as to means, and knew when to compromise. A natural dramatist, he was able to project his personal charm both in public appearances and in those radio "fireside chats" in which he seemed to be taking the whole country into his confidence. Thus he won loyalty to his ideals as well as to his person.

Indispensable to Roosevelt's well-being and success was Mrs. Roosevelt, whom the whole country before long was calling by her first name. Franklin found traveling difficult, but Eleanor went everywhere, by car, train, and airplane, even to Pacific Ocean bases during World War II. She visited and talked to all sorts and conditions of people, giving them a feeling that the government really cared about them. She took a particular interest in the disoriented and confused young people then graduating from schools and colleges, and was instrumental in preventing thousands of them from going Red [i.e., becoming Communists]. Among the colored people she became a legendary benefactress; and, in so doing, alienated the white South. She maintained the atmosphere of a gentleman's country home in the White House, amid all the hurlyburly of the New Deal. But she never intruded upon or tried to influence the President's policy. . . .

The New Dealers and Their Quirks

Roosevelt's first cabinet included two men over sixty: Cordell Hull, secretary of state who had been congressman and senator from Tennessee for thirty years, and William H. Woodin, secretary of the treasury, who came of a family of Pennsylvania ironmasters. Others were James A. Farley, who had expertly managed the campaign and thus received the postmaster-generalship, chief source of patronage; Henry A. Wallace, second-generation editor of a farm journal and the world's greatest authority on hybrid corn, secretary of agriculture; Harold L. Ickes, elderly, peppery . . . conservationist from Chicago, secretary of the interior; and Frances Perkins, social worker from New York, secretary of labor. There was something odd about every one of these except Hull, a Southern statesman of the old school, and Farley, a typical Irish Democrat. Woodin played the guitar and composed songs; Wallace was a religious mystic; Ickes had a persecution complex; and [as for] . . . "Madam" Perkins, as she was called, . . . it was odd to have a woman in the cabinet, especially in the labor office. Several members were former Republicans. . . .

Roosevelt had the same facility as Lincoln in profiting from the expertise of his advisers while overlooking their quirks; he could use the slow, ruminating mind of a Hull as well as the brittle cleverness of a Bill Bullitt. Raymond Moley of Ohio, professor of public law at Columbia, and Rexford G. Tugwell, professor of economics in the same university, became respectively assistant secretaries of state and agriculture; several others with a similar professorial background were highly placed.

Many of the unofficial cabinet, the "brain-trusters" whom Roosevelt brought to Washington, were more important than the real cabinet. Harry Hopkins, son of a Mid-Western harness maker, was the most brainy, whether in social welfare matters in which he had been trained, or in later war issues which were completely new to him. [British statesman] Winston Churchill once called Hopkins "Mr. Root of the Matter," because he had an astonishing ability to get to the bottom of a problem in the shortest time. Thomas C. "Tommy the Cork" Corcoran, with his quick mind and Irish wit, and Benjamin Cohen, quiet, scholarly, and thorough, were an important part of the setup. Collectively the "New Dealers," within and without the cabinet, were well educated, at home in the world of ideas, talkers and discussers, eager to put their intelligence to the service of the government.

A New Deal of Old Cards

"I pledge you, I pledge myself, to a New Deal for the American people," said Roosevelt in his speech accepting the Democratic nomination. That theme, which he returned to frequently during the campaign, gave a collective name to his policies—the New Deal. The series of measures that he inaugurated was a natural development from his cousin's [President Theodore Roosevelt's] Square Deal and [President Woodrow] Wilson's New Freedom. The only really new thing about it was a conscious effort, through legislation, to enhance the welfare and eventual security of simple folk throughout the country. These, at his accession, felt completely helpless, humiliated by the business and financial barons who had deceived them, and neglected by the previous administrations.

The transfer of wealth from the rich to the poor by government action had been suggested by Theodore Roosevelt in his Bull Moose campaign; and the income and inheritance taxes now made it possible. This policy, which Roosevelt and the Democrats pursued relentlessly, led to what was named, in scorn, the Welfare State. It did not prevent rewards to the skill and organizing ability of able individuals, as the increase of great fortunes since World War II has proved; but it vastly increased the power of organized labor and gave the ordinary citizen a feeling of financial security against old age, sickness, and unemployment which he had never enjoyed, and a participation in government such as he had never felt since Lincoln's era. At the same time a large part of the middle class, especially those who had retired on pensions or annuities, felt squeezed between the upper and nether millstones.

Thus the New Deal was just what the term implied—a new deal of old cards, no longer stacked against the common man. Opponents called it near-fascism or near-communism, but it was American as a bale of hay—an opportunist, rule-of-thumb method of curing deep-seated ills. Probably it saved the capitalist system in the United States; there is no knowing what might have happened under another administration like Hoover's. The German Republic fell before Hitler largely because it kept telling the people, "The government can do nothing for you." And, as proof that the Roosevelt administration was trying to avoid excessive governmental power rather than promote socialism, in his very first measure, the Banking Act, the President refused to consider nationalization. He insisted on leaving the banks free and independent. . . . The New Deal seemed newer than it really was, partly because progressive principles had largely been forgotten for thirteen years, but mostly because the cards were dealt with such bewildering rapidity.

Roosevelt Forms the "Brain Trust"

Ted Morgan

This essay by Ted Morgan, author of well-received bi-
ographies of statesmen Franklin Roosevelt and Winston
Churchill, provides an excellent introduction to the members of Roosevelt's "Brain Trust." This was the nickname
for the small group of intellectuals, mostly college acade-
mics, that became some of the new president's closest advisors. Having suddenly been thrust into the highest corridors of political power, these little-known nonelected
officials, including Raymond Moley, Rex Tugwell, and
Adolf Berle, ended up having a profound influence on the
course of the New Deal and, through it, the country's economic and social development.

Roosevelt was still governor [of New York state], absorbed in
state matters, with 800 bills to sign at the end of the legislative session, and had to run his campaign as well. He didn't
have time to study the national issues. He couldn't simply
apply his knowledge of the state to the nation. His mail told
him there was a breakdown in the system, and that old ap-
proaches were futile. But as to how to fix it, he was no economist. His competence on every topic of national concern
was going to be tested in the campaign, and he wasn't ready.
He had to rise above the Lippmann view that he was no more
than an amiable fellow who wanted to be president. He
needed tutoring, but the men around him, aside from Sam
Rosenman [one of his key advisors], weren't much help. . . .

Rosenman brought it up one evening in March: "If you
were to be nominated tomorrow and had to start a campaign

Reprinted with the permission of Simon & Schuster, Inc., from *FDR: A Biography*,
by Ted Morgan. Copyright ©1985 by Ted Morgan.

trip within ten days, we'd be in an awful fix. You would be without a well-defined and thought-out affirmative program. It would be pretty hard to get up intelligent speeches overnight on the many subjects you would have to discuss. . . . My thought is that if we can get a small group together willing to give some time, they can prepare memoranda about such things as the relief of agriculture, tariffs, railroads, government debts, private credit, money, gold standard—all the things you will have to take a definite stand on. . . . The first one I thought I would talk with is Ray Moley. He believes in your social philosophy and objectives, and he has a clear and forceful style of writing. Being a university professor himself, he can suggest different university people in different fields. Is that all right with you?"

A Gift for Putting Ideas into Words

Moley, the first member of what came to be known as the "brain trust," had already done some work for Roosevelt. . . . His hostility toward international bankers and "fat cat" Republicans came from his Ohio background. Born in 1886 in Berea, where his father had a "gents' furnishings" store, he grew up a passionate admirer of [orator and unsuccessful presidential candidate] William Jennings Bryan and of Cleveland's progressive mayor, Tom L. Johnson. His bible was single-tax advocate Henry George's *Progress and Poverty*. A professor at Columbia, Moley was eager for public service and served on a commission to revise the parole laws under Roosevelt. Moley at first thought Roosevelt's amiability was "be good to the peasants" stuff, but came to realize that he genuinely enjoyed being open and friendly—he was conscious of his ability to send callers away happy and glowing, often having forgotten what they had come to ask. A typical approach to big problems was "so and so was telling me today"—there was complete freedom from dogmatism, a case-by-case approach, a fluid mind. The frightening aspect was his grand receptivity; he made no attempt to check up on anything anyone told him.

Moley had a gift for putting into words Roosevelt's half-formulated ideas, and carved out a position of eminence, which Rosenman resented. Rosenman came to see Moley as "a very ambitious man, very devious in some of his dealings." He was offended by Moley's remark that it was because of Rosenman's "boyish love" of Columbia that all the members of the brain trust came from there. The fact was he had little love of Columbia, having spent unhappy years there when Jews were social outcasts. The reason he wanted Columbia men was purely practical: Roosevelt had no funds to pay the expenses of a professor from the University of California or even from Yale. He had to draw on men living in the city who could come to meetings on a nickel subway fare.

James P. Warburg, who was assistant secretary of the Treasury in the first Roosevelt administration, believed that Moley's attraction to Roosevelt was almost physical. "He was a man in whom homo and heterosexuality was curiously in balance," Warburg said. "He 'fell for' men the way a man falls for a woman. He seemed to have a great need to make a series of friendships with men. I don't mean by this that he was or is an overt homosexual at all. The pattern seemed to be one of making these friendships and being betrayed by one after another. . . . It always seemed to end up with the favorite of today becoming the disloyal betrayer of tomorrow. . . . He idealized Roosevelt and Roosevelt, in a psychological sense, was his 'dream girl.' And thus Moley became his very humble worshiper and servant."

The Chance to Become an Insider

On a blustery March morning, Moley ran into economics professor Rexford Guy Tugwell on Morningside Heights, near Columbia University. Moley thought Tugwell was politically naive, but he was an expert on agriculture. He liked Tugwell, who was handsome and brilliant—his conversation was like a cocktail, it picked you up and made your brain race along. He asked Rex if he would be willing to advise Roosevelt. Tugwell, who could see the Hooverville [community of makeshift shacks] spreading across the tracks from Columbia, had formed the habit of indulging immoderate remarks about the president. This was a chance to do something, to be an insider, to influence policy, to have the words he had written spoken before a large audience. "I was just a fellow who was pretty mad and thought he saw some things that could be done," he recalled.

Then forty-one, Tugwell came from Sinclairsville in western New York, where his father owned a farm and a cannery. He graduated from the Wharton School of Finance and Commerce at the University of Pennsylvania, and mingled with the socialists of the League of Industrial Democracy. In 1927, he spent two months in Soviet Russia with a delegation of trade unionists and intellectuals. Impressed by the renewal of Soviet agriculture, he wondered whether there might be an alternative to the boom-and-bust cycle of laissez-faire capitalism. "How shall we settle our irrepressible agricultural problem except by some such series of devices as the Soviets use?" he asked. He rejected Soviet political doctrine, but wanted to adapt some of their economic practices, such as long-range centralized planning and crop limitations. He commented that "if Communism is a religion, capitalism is a fetish." But he made this distinction between liberals and radicals: "Liberals would like to rebuild the station while the trains are running; radicals prefer to blow up the station and forgo service until the new structure is built."

A "Walking Mind"

Moley had been impressed by a young colleague at meetings devoted to curriculum revisions at the Columbia University Law School. He was sharp and clever and knew a lot about finance—indeed, he was coauthoring a book on the nature of the modern corporation. He would fit right in. But when approached, the colleague, Adolf A. Berle, Jr., told Moley that he supported [rival candidate] Newton D. Baker. That was all right, Moley said, it was his technical expertise that was wanted, not his political support, which did not carry the slightest weight in any case. Berle laughed and signed on, although he continued to work for Baker as well.

Berle was born in the Boston suburb of Brighton in 1895. His grandfather was a German immigrant, his father was a Congregational minister, and his mother was the daughter of another Congregationalist minister who had done missionary work with the Sioux in South Dakota. From his father and his maternal grandfather, he had examples of religious vocations combined with social activism. His father was a reformer, preaching the social gospel, the rights of children to finish high school and not be sent to work when they were four-teen, the need for a basic economic reorganization. Berle grew up believing that with proper guidance the system could be made to work. Tutored at home, he entered Harvard when he was fourteen, and graduated in three years with honors. He had his Harvard Law School degree by the time he was twenty-one. In the World War he was a pacifist. . . . But in 1917 he enlisted in the Signal Corps. After that, he taught law at Harvard and Columbia, becoming an expert on large corporations and how they challenged the power of the state.

Berle was delighted by Roosevelt because he was not hide-bound or orthodox. He was prepared to look at an idea on its merits and adopt it. But you had to present it in a way that he could use. Once they brought in the economist James W. An-gell, who knew more about money than anyone. Roosevelt asked him if they should change the gold content of the dol-lar. Angell said the question was too complicated to answer off the bat. "Well, we obviously aren't going to have any huge amount of time for research," Roosevelt said. "These prob-lems are going to be presented right quick."

"Well, to estimate the effects of what would happen is going to be very difficult," Angell cautioned.

"Listen, Jim," Roosevelt said, "I'm a ham and eggs politi-cian, and you're an authority on monetary matters. Forget about your academic reputation . . . just tell me, if you had to guess what it would be."

"You know, I really don't think I could take the responsi-bility of making a guess," Angell said.

That was the end of him, Berle recalled. But Berle made the grade, although Moley sometimes regretted bringing him in because he was so arrogant and self-centered. It was Moley who said that he may have been an infant prodigy, but he continued to be an infant long after he had ceased to be a prodigy. Rex Tugwell said that Berle was a "walking mind," but not a modest one.

The Aroma of Power

Despite the personality clashes, the brain trust worked. Roosevelt liked to gather the professors around him and pick their brains. They were young and intense world changers, smelling the heady aroma of power for the first time, plucked from the classroom and given a golden opportunity to implement their ideas. Tugwell felt that they were turning weakness into competence, leading an agile mind to higher levels of discussion. They were tailors conducting fittings, cutting the cloth to the pattern, trying it on, letting it out here and tucking it in there.

The first major collaboration was a ten-minute speech Roosevelt was due to deliver on April 7 over network radio on the "Lucky Strike Hour," sponsored by the American Tobacco Company. Moley wrote it, remembering the phrase "forgotten man" from an essay by the Yale economist William Graham Sumner, who had used it to designate the middle class. But Moley applied it to the disadvantaged lower third of the population. Roosevelt compared the depression to the World War, when the nation had mobilized its resources to win. The same mobilization was needed now. Public works were not enough. The government must not only lend money at the top, as it was doing through Hoover's Reconstruction Finance Corporation, but should prevent mortgage foreclosures on farmers and homeowners. It must put its faith once more in "the forgotten man at the bottom of the economic pyramid." This was hardly earthshaking, but it announced a new direction.

The Historic "Hundred Days"

William E. Leuchtenburg

"The most extraordinary series of reforms in the nation's history" is how William E. Leuchtenburg, former Columbia University scholar and one of the foremost experts on the depression era, describes the opening salvo of the New Deal. In the following synopsis, Leuchtenburg tells how, during the first legislative session of his presidency, incoming president Franklin Roosevelt swiftly and firmly guided Congress through the process of debating and passing a flurry of wide-ranging major reform bills.

"First of all," declared the new President, "let me assert my firm belief that the only thing we have to fear is fear itself—nameless, unreasoning, unjustified terror. . . ." Grim, unsmiling, chin uplifted, his voice firm, almost angry, he lashed out at the bankers. "We are stricken by no plague of locusts. . . . Plenty is at our doorstep, but a generous use of it languishes in the very sight of the supply. Primarily this is because rulers of the exchange of mankind's goods have failed through their own stubbornness and their own incompetence, have admitted their failure, and have abdicated. . . . The money changers have fled from their high seats in the temple of our civilization. We may now restore that temple to the ancient truths."

The nation, Roosevelt insisted, must move "as a trained and loyal army willing to sacrifice for the good of a common discipline." He would go to Congress with a plan of action, but if Congress did not act and the emergency persisted, the President announced, "I shall not evade the clear course of duty that will then confront me. I shall ask the Congress for the one remaining instrument to meet the crisis—broad Ex-

Excerpted from *Franklin D. Roosevelt and the New Deal, 1932–1940*, New American Nation Series, by William E. Leuchtenburg. Reprinted by permission of Harper-Collins Publishers, Inc.

ecutive power to wage a war against the emergency, as great as the power that would be given to me if we were in fact invaded by a foreign foe."

In the main part of his Inaugural Address, his program for recovery, he had little new to offer. What he did say was so vague as to be open to any interpretation. . . . Yet this was a new Roosevelt; the air of casual gaiety, of evasiveness, had vanished—the ring of his voice, the swing of his shoulders, his call for sacrifice, discipline, and action demonstrated he was a man confident in his powers as leader of the nation. In declaring there was nothing to fear but fear, Roosevelt had minted no new platitude; Hoover had said the same thing repeatedly for three years. Yet Roosevelt had nonetheless made his greatest single contribution to the politics of the 1930's: the instillation of hope and courage in the people. He made clear that the time of waiting was over, that he had the people's interests at heart, and that he would mobilize the power of the government to help them. In the next week, nearly half a million Americans wrote their new President. He had made an impression which Hoover had never been able to create—of a man who knew how to lead and had faith in the future.

The Bank Holiday

Roosevelt moved swiftly to deal with the financial illness that paralyzed the nation. On his very first night in office, he directed Secretary of the Treasury William Woodin to draft an emergency banking bill, and gave him less than five days to get it ready. Woodin found the Treasury corridors prey to rumor, the bankers empty of ideas and queasy with fear of new calamities. To buy Woodin time to prepare legislation, and to protect the nation's dwindling gold reserves, Roosevelt assumed the posture of a commander in chief in wartime. On Sunday afternoon, March 5, he approved the issue of two presidential edicts—one called Congress into special session on March 9; the other, resting on the rather doubtful legal authority of the Trading with the Enemy Act of 1917, halted transactions in gold and proclaimed a national bank holiday.

The very totality of the bank holiday helped snap the tension the country had been under all winter. "Holiday" was a delightful euphemism, and the nation, responding in good spirit, devised ingenious ways to make life go on as it always had. In Michigan, Canadian money circulated; in the South-west, Mexican pesos; the Dow Chemical Company paid its workers in coins made of Dowmetal, a magnesium alloy. . . .

On March 9, the special session of Congress convened in an atmosphere of wartime crisis. Shortly before 1 P.M., Roosevelt's banking message was read, while some newly elected congressmen were still trying to find their seats. The House had no copies of the bill; the Speaker recited the text from the one available draft, which bore last-minute corrections scribbled in pencil. Members found the proposal an exceptionally conservative document. Roosevelt's assault on the bankers in his inaugural address had invited speculation that he might advocate radical reforms, even nationalization of the banks. Instead, the emergency banking measure extended government assistance to private bankers to reopen their banks. The bill validated actions the President had already taken, gave him complete control over gold movements, penalized hoarding, authorized the issue of new Federal Reserve bank notes, and arranged for the reopening of banks with liquid assets and the reorganization of the rest. . . .

With a unanimous shout, the House passed the bill, sight unseen, after only thirty-eight minutes of debate. . . . The Senate, over the objections of a small band of progressives, approved the bill unamended 73–7 at 7:30 that evening and at 8:36 that same night it received the President's signature. . . .

On Sunday night, March 12, an estimated sixty million people sat around radio sets to hear the first of President Roosevelt's "fireside chats." In warmly comforting tones, the President assured the nation it was now safe to return their savings to the banks. The next morning, banks opened their doors in the twelve Federal Reserve Bank cities. Nothing so much indicated the sharp shift in public sentiment as the fact that people were now more eager to deposit cash than to withdraw it. . . . Deprived of cash for several days, people had been expected to withdraw funds to meet immediate needs, yet in every city deposits far exceeded withdrawals. The crisis was over. "Capitalism," Raymond Moley [one of Roosevelt's chief advisors] later concluded, "was saved in eight days."

The Economy Bill and Repeal of Prohibition

On March 10, Roosevelt fired his second message at Congress. He requested sweeping powers to slice $400 million from payments to veterans and to slash the pay of federal employees another $100 million. "Too often in recent history," the President warned, "liberal governments have been wrecked on rocks of loose fiscal policy." The economy bill reflected the influence of Director of the Budget Lewis Douglas, who thought that Hoover had indulged in "wild extravagance." Convinced that the proposal echoed the demand of Wall Street for wage slashing and that it was cruel to veterans, the Democratic caucus in the House refused to support the President. One congressman protested that the bill would benefit "big powerful banking racketeers," while another called it "a slaughter of the disabled servicemen of the United States." At any other time, such appeals would have carried both chambers, but they made little headway against the power of the President in a time of crisis. . . . Although more than ninety Democrats broke with Roosevelt in the House, most of them heeded [Virginia congressman Clifton] Woodrum's counsel. After only two days' debate, Congress passed the economy bill. Under the leadership of Franklin Roosevelt, the budget balancers had won a victory for orthodox finance that had not been possible under Hoover.

The staccato rhythm of the Hundred Days had begun: on Thursday, Congress adopted the bank bill; on Saturday, it passed the economy measure; on Monday, March 13, the President asked Congress to fulfill the Democratic pledge of an early end to prohibition. Roosevelt's victory had speeded a remarkable revolution in sentiment; even some veteran dry congressmen now voted for liquor. In February, 1933, the wets had broken a fainthearted Senate filibuster, and the lame-duck Congress, in a startling reversal of attitude, voted to repeal the Eighteenth Amendment [which had prohibited alcohol]. While the Twenty-first Amendment [ending Prohibition] was making its way through the states, Roosevelt requested quick action to amend the Volstead Act by legalizing beer of 3.2 per cent alcoholic content by weight.

Roosevelt's message touched off a raucous, rollicking debate. The drys, who had succeeded in killing a beer bill only a few weeks before, rehearsed the arguments that had been so convincing for more than a decade, but to no avail. Representative John Boylan of New York protested that this was "the same old sob story you have been telling us for the last 12 years. Why, I almost know your words verbatim—the distressed mother, the wayward son, the unruly daughter, the roadhouse, and so forth, and so forth. . . ." Impatient congressmen chanted: "Vote—vote—we want beer"; within a week both houses had passed the beer bill, and added wine for good measure, although congressmen protested that 3.2 wine was not "interesting." On March 22, Roosevelt signed the bill. . . .

Debate over a Farm Bill

Two weeks after Roosevelt took office, the country seemed a changed place. Where once there had been apathy and despondency, there was now an immense sense of movement. If the country did not know in what direction it was moving, it had great expectations; the spell of lassitude [listlessness] had been snapped. On the walls of Thomas A. Edison, Inc., in West Orange, New Jersey, President Charles Edison posted a notice:

> President Roosevelt has done his part: now you do something.
>
> Buy something—buy anything, anywhere; paint your kitchen, send a telegram, give a party, get a car, pay a bill, rent a flat, fix your roof, get a haircut, see a show, build a house, take a trip, sing a song, get married.
>
> It does not matter what you do—but get going and keep going. This old world is starting to move. . . .

Roosevelt had originally planned a quick session of Congress which would adjourn as soon as it had dealt with the banking crisis, but it responded so well to his first proposals that he decided to hold it in session. On March 16, the

President charted a new course by sending his farm message to Congress.

In framing a farm bill, Secretary of Agriculture Henry Wallace preferred the "domestic allotment" plan . . . [which] aimed to deal with the crucial problem of depressed prices and mounting surpluses. Hoover's Farm Board had tried to raise prices without curbing production, only to see a half-billion dollars go down the drain with no substantial benefit to farmers. . . . Advocates of the domestic allotment plan proposed to restrict acreage; levy a tax on the processors of agricultural commodities (for example, the miller who converted wheat into flour); and pay farmers who agreed to limit production benefits based on "parity," which would give the farmer the same level of purchasing power he had had before the war.

Roosevelt had his own ideas about a satisfactory farm program—he disliked dumping, wanted decentralized administration, and stipulated the plan should obtain the consent of a majority of the farmers—but, above all, he insisted that farm leaders themselves agree on the kind of bill they wanted. In this fashion, he avoided antagonizing farm spokesmen by choosing one device in preference to another, and threw the responsibility for achieving a workable solution on the farm organizations. . . . They were willing to bargain and so was the administration. Wallace, who wanted a farm act before planting time, proposed an omnibus bill which would embody different alternatives, and that, after a series of conferences with farm spokesmen, was what he got.

The House quickly passed the farm bill without change, but the Senate balked at speedy action. The measure shocked conservatives and drew the wrath of lobbyists for the processors—millers, packers, canners, and others—who objected to the proposed processing tax. At the same time, the radical wing of the farm movement protested that the farmer deserved nothing less than government guarantee of his "cost of production.". . .

The Gold Standard and the Farm Bill

On April 18, Senate leaders warned Roosevelt that a new inflationary amendment to the farm bill, sponsored by Senator

Elmer Thomas of Oklahoma, could not be defeated. Recognizing that the situation would soon be out of hand, Roosevelt decided to accept the Thomas proposal if it was rewritten to give the President discretionary powers rather than making any specific course of inflationary action mandatory. In its revised form, the Thomas amendment authorized the President to bring about inflation through remonetizing silver, printing greenbacks, or altering the gold content of the dollar. . . .

The following day, Roosevelt, confined in bed by a sore throat, announced with a smile to the 125 newspapermen gathered in his bedroom that the United States was off the gold standard. The country had, to be sure, been on a greatly modified gold basis for some weeks. The President wrote later of an encounter with Secretary Woodin on April 20: "His face was wreathed in smiles, but I looked at him and said: 'Mr. Secretary, I have some very bad news for you. I have to announce to you the serious fact that the United States has gone off the gold standard.' Mr. Woodin is a good sport. He threw up both hands, opened his eyes wide and exclaimed: 'My heavens! What, again?'" Yet Roosevelt's embargo of the export of gold represented a decisive turn—nothing less than the jettisoning of the international gold standard.

Roosevelt took the country off gold, not simply to forestall the inflationists, but because he was deeply concerned by the deflation of the first six weeks of the New Deal. By going off gold, he sought to free himself to engage in domestic price-raising ventures. The President's action horrified conservatives. . . . But Roosevelt's historic decision won applause not only from farm-state senators but, unexpectedly, from the House of [noted financier J.P.] Morgan. Morgan himself publicly announced his approval, and Russell Leffingwell [Morgan's partner] wrote the President: "Your action in going off gold saved the country from complete collapse. It was vitally necessary and the most important of all helpful things you have done."

As Congress continued to wrangle over the farm bill, rebellion once more broke out in the Corn Belt. In late April, a mob of farmers, masked in blue bandannas, dragged Judge

Charles C. Bradley from his bench in LeMars, Iowa, took him to a crossroads out of town, and nearly lynched him in a vain effort to get him to promise not to sign mortgage foreclosures. A few days later, to force the hand of Congress, the Farmers' Holiday Association . . . called a national farmers' strike for May 13.

On May 12, racing to nip the farm strike in the bud, Congress passed the Agricultural Adjustment Act. Since it provided for alternative systems of subsidizing farm staples, the law simply postponed the quarrel over farm policy; within a few months, it would erupt again. But for the moment farm leaders were content to count their blessings. The act gave the farmer the price supports he desired, and more besides. The Thomas amendment held out to the debt-ridden farmer the prospect of freshly printed greenbacks; the supplementary Farm Credit Act of June 16 promised to keep the sheriff and the mortgage company away from his door. Within eighteen months, the Farm Credit Administration, a merger of government farm loan agencies under the energetic Henry Morgenthau, Jr., and his deputy, William Myers of Cornell, would refinance a fifth of all farm mortgages. After more than a half century of agitation, the farmer had come into his own.

The CCC and HOLC

By the spring of 1933, the needs of more than fifteen million unemployed had quite overwhelmed the resources of local governments. In some counties, as many as 90 per cent of the people were on relief. Roosevelt was not indifferent to the plea of mayors and county commissioners for federal assistance, but the relief proposal closest to his heart had more special aims: the creation of a civilian forest army to put the "wild boys of the road" and the unemployed of the cities to work in the national forests. On March 14, the President asked four of his cabinet to consider the conservation corps idea, a project which united his belief in universal service for youth with his desire to improve the nation's estate. Moreover, Roosevelt thought that the character of city men would benefit from a furlough in the country. The next day, his officials reported back with a recommendation not only for tree-army legislation but for public works and federal grants to the states for relief. . . . On March 21, the President sent an unemployment relief message to Congress which embraced all three recommendations. Congress took only eight days to create the Civilian Conservation Corps. In little more than a week, the Senate whipped through a bill authorizing half a billion dollars in direct federal grants to the states for relief, and the House gave its approval three weeks later. . . .

Especially critical was the plight of homeowners. In 1932, a quarter of a million families lost their homes. In the first half of 1933, more than a thousand homes were being foreclosed every day; Philadelphia averaged 1,300 sheriff's sales a month. In June, Congress adopted the Home Owners' Loan Act amidst cries that the law bailed out real-estate interests rather than the homeowner. Without having to scale down the debt he was owed, the mortgagor could turn in defaulted mortgages for guaranteed government bonds. Yet, however much the act was tailored to the interests of financial institutions, it proved a lifesaver for thousands of Americans. When the Home Owners' Loan Corporation opened for business in Akron, a double column stretched for three blocks down Main Street by seven in the morning; when the doors opened, five hundred people pressed into the lobby. In the end, the HOLC would help refinance one out of every five mortgaged urban private dwellings in America.

The TVA and NIRA

As Roosevelt followed one startling recommendation for reform legislation with yet another, the progressive bloc in Congress came to the pleasant realization that all kinds of proposals that had been doomed to defeat for more than a decade now had an excellent chance of adoption. Of all the projects espoused by the Republican progressives, one in particular symbolized their frustration during the recent reign of three Republican Presidents. Led by George Norris of Nebraska, the progressives had fought year in and year out for government operation of the Muscle Shoals properties on the Tennessee River, an electric power and nitrogen development built during World War I. Twice Congress had passed a Muscle Shoals bill; twice it had been killed by Republican Presidents. Now the progressives found an ally in the new Democratic President. . . .

On April 10, the President asked Congress to create the Tennessee Valley Authority. The TVA would build multipurpose dams which would serve as reservoirs to control floods and at the same time generate cheap, abundant hydroelectric power. Its power operations were designed to serve as a "yardstick" to measure what would be reasonable rates for a power company to charge. The Authority, which would be a public corporation with the powers of government but the flexibility of a private corporation, would manufacture fertilizer, dig a 650-mile navigation channel from Knoxville to Paducah, engage in soil conservation and reforestation, and, to the gratification of the planners, cooperate with state and local agencies in social experiments. . . . The House passed the measure by a whopping margin; Norris steered it through the Senate; and, after he had first made sure that congressional conferees had approved his more ambitious conception of the project, Franklin Roosevelt signed the Tennessee Valley Authority Act on May 18.

While Roosevelt had sent an impressive number of legislative proposals to Congress, he had still done nothing directly to stimulate industrial recovery. . . . The most popular of all [industrial] proposals arose from the plea of such business leaders as Gerard Swope of General Electric and Henry I. Harriman of the U.S. Chamber of Commerce that the government suspend the antitrust laws to permit trade associations to engage in industrywide planning. . . . A number of union leaders, especially men like John L. Lewis and Sidney Hillman in the sick coal and garment industries, had [also] come to believe that only by national action could their industries be stabilized. They were willing to agree to business proposals for a suspension of the antitrust laws because they assumed the Supreme Court would not sanction a federal wages and hours law, and they reasoned that industrial codes offered high-wage businessmen badly needed protection from operators who connived to undersell them by exploiting their workers. But Senator Wagner, the most eloquent champion of the rights of labor in Congress, insisted that if business received concessions labor must have a guarantee of collective bargaining.

On May 10, out of patience with the wrangling over the industrial recovery bill, Roosevelt named a drafting committee and told the draftsmen to lock themselves in a room and not come out until they had a bill. A week later, the President was able to present Congress with an omnibus proposal that had a little for everyone. Business got government authorization to draft code agreements exempt from the antitrust laws; the planners won their demand for government licensing of business; and labor received Section 7(a), modeled on War Labor Board practices, which guaranteed the right to collective bargaining and stipulated that the codes should set minimum wages and maximum hours. In addition, the bill provided for $3.3 billion in public works. . . .

On June 16, when President Roosevelt signed the National Industrial Recovery Act, he observed: "Many good men voted this new charter with misgivings. I do not share these doubts. I had part in the great cooperation of 1917 and 1918 and it is my faith that we can count on our industry once more to join in our general purpose to lift this new threat.". . .

History in the Making

When Congress adjourned on June 16, precisely one hundred days after the special session opened, it had written into the laws of the land the most extraordinary series of reforms in the nation's history. It had committed the country to an unprecedented program of government-industry cooperation; promised to distribute stupendous sums to millions of staple farmers; accepted responsibility for the welfare of millions of unemployed; agreed to engage in far-reaching experimentation in regional planning; pledged billions of dollars to save homes and farms from foreclosure; undertaken huge public works spending; guaranteed the small bank deposits of the country; and had, for the first time, established federal regulation of Wall Street. The next day, as the President sat at his desk in the White House signing several of the bills Congress had adopted, including the largest peacetime appropriation bill ever passed, he remarked: "More history is being made today than in [any] one day of our national life." Oklahoma's Senator Thomas Gore amended: "During all time."

Roosevelt had directed the entire operation like a seasoned field general. He had sent fifteen messages up to the Hill, seen fifteen historic laws through to final passage. Supremely confident, every inch the leader, he dumbfounded his critics of a few months before. "Roosevelt the Candidate and Roosevelt the President are two different men," observed a veteran newspaperman. "I assert as much, for I am well acquainted with both. In the first role he was famous for his beguiling smile, famous for his soft words, famous for his punchless speeches. . . . The oath of office seems suddenly to have transfigured him from a man of mere charm and buoyancy to one of dynamic aggressiveness." Others conceded that they might have been mistaken. . . . Republican editor and Socialist writer, G.O.P. senators and progressive critics, all shared in a common rejoicing. The nation, at last, had found a leader.

Chapter 4

New Deal Programs, Policies, and Controversies

Turning Points

IN WORLD HISTORY

The SEC Regulates Wall Street

Mario Einaudi

Today, both current stockholders and first-time stock investors take for granted numerous rules that discourage fraudulent trading practices and make investing in the stock market, while still a risk, at least fair to all. Before Franklin Roosevelt took office, however, Wall Street was not regulated, which to an arguable degree contributed to the rampant speculation that caused the 1929 crash. One of the major accomplishments of the New Deal was the creation of the Securities and Exchange Commission (SEC). As the late political scholar Mario Einaudi explains in this excerpt from his informative book *The Roosevelt Revolution*, the SEC, established in 1934, strictly regulates the practices of firms, brokers, and the stock exchange itself, providing the public a significant measure of protection.

The Great Depression had found in Wall Street its representative symbol, so the New Deal made of it the object of particularly tender care. There were not only specific abuses and misuses of economic power to be corrected. It was quite likely that on the Wall Street front a basic test of power would have to be faced by the American government. The Securities and Exchange Commission was conceived, therefore, as one of the most powerful and careful devices for the vindication of the purposes of the new state. The SEC is today entrusted with the enforcement of a long series of legislative enactments that became effective over a seven-year period from 1933 to 1940, as the persistence and the continuity of New Deal reforms in this field never relented.

In signing the last of these major pieces of legislation on August 23, 1940, Roosevelt said, in words which render in-

Excerpted from *The Roosevelt Revolution*, by Mario Einaudi. Copyright ©1959 and renewed 1987 by Mario Einaudi. Adapted by permission of Harcourt Inc.

credibly tenuous the argument that, as a result of the advent of World War II, an interruption or even a repudiation of the New Deal occurred:

> As the pressure of international affairs increases, we are ready for the emergency because of our vigorous fight to put our domestic affairs on a true democratic basis. We are cleaning house, putting our financial machinery in good order. This program is essential, not only because it results in necessary reforms, but for the much more important reason that it will enable us to absorb the shock of any crisis.

Full Disclosure

The SEC has a dominant jurisdiction in four major areas of the financial life of the United States.

In the first place, the SEC administers the Securities Act of 1933, requiring the full disclosure to investors of all essential facts concerning securities publicly offered for sale. Disclosure is secured by requiring the issuer to file with the Commission a registration statement and a prospectus containing all significant information, favorable or unfavorable, about the issuer and the securities offered for sale. These documents are available for public inspection as soon as they are filed, and a waiting period of twenty days is usually required before the securities can be sold. The Commission can refuse to grant registration if it discovers elements of fraud and deceit in the registration statements during these twenty days. The Commission has the right to send out to the registrant so-called deficiency letters whenever the examination of the registration statement discloses omissions or incomplete statements of central facts. This procedure can lead to the withdrawal or the stopping of the registration. On the other hand, if the registration statement is cleared by the Commission, the clearance does not imply approval or disapproval by the Commission of the securities in question. It merely indicates that the issuer has complied with the full-disclosure requirements of the Act, so that the investor himself is in a good position to measure the risks involved in any purchase of the securities in question. The two chief weapons of the Commission are publicity and the right to stop the issue if adequate disclosure of all the facts is not forthcoming.

Fair Trading and Investment Policies

The second major area is the administration of the Securities Exchange Act of 1934, regulating the operations of the stock exchanges themselves. The Act is designed to insure the integrity and fairness of trading operations on the organized exchanges and on the over-the-counter market. The Act undertakes to eliminate abuses in security trading. It requires that full information concerning securities that are admitted to trading on a stock exchange shall be made available to the public. It also regulates and limits the use of credit in security dealings. . . .

Next, the SEC administers the Investment Company Act and the Investment Advisers Act of 1940. The Investment Company Act provides for the registration and regulation of all investment trusts. It requires the disclosure of the investment policies of these companies, prohibits them from changing the nature of their business or their investment policies without the approval of their stockholders, regulates the custody of the company's assets, requires management credit checks to be submitted to security holders for their approval, prohibits transactions between the companies and their officers and directors except with the approval of the Commission.

The Investment Advisers Act requires the registration of those who are engaged for compensation in the business of advising others with respect to securities. The Commission is empowered to deny registration or revoke the registration of any investment adviser who, after notice and opportunity for hearing, is found by the Commission to have a record of misconduct in connection with security transactions or to have made false statements in his application for registration. The Act makes it unlawful for investment advisers to engage in practices which constitute fraud or deceit and requires advisers to disclose the nature of their interest in transactions executed for their clients.

Finally, the SEC administers the Public Utilities Holding Company Act of 1935 [which streamlined and regulated the financial practices of large electric and gas companies]. This alone would more than justify its existence, since the Act has brought about a permanent readjustment of economic power in one of the vital sectors of American economic life. . . .

Politics Over Economics

The scope and detail of these powers are impressive. Their justification is found in the damage done by the financial community to the American economy and to the American public in the years that preceded the Great Depression. It is found in the scandalous practices uncovered by public investigation of the activities of stockbrokers and stock exchanges. It is found in the instances of outright looting on a massive scale of the assets of investment trusts and other companies whose securities were being sold to a public ignorant of the deceit and fraud practiced with notable imagination and daring.

Until 1932, Wall Street leaders had been in the habit of making extravagant claims for themselves. They had attempted to assume powers that could not properly belong to them and they had identified themselves as the mainstay of an ever-improving level of prosperity and economic growth. When these claims were found to be hollow, and when the power was claimed on behalf of the people of the United States by the new agencies of government of the New Deal, the regulations adopted acquired a severity that was proportional to the gravity of the issue.

Here, perhaps more clearly than anywhere else, did the New Deal assert the primacy of politics over economics, the right of the community to regulate private activities undertaken for purposes of gain, in order to see that the public interest as well as the interest of other private citizens would not be damaged. Even from the point of view of classical liberalism, the setting of the rules of important games is a primary function of public power. In the United States, playing with money, other people's money, had become an exceedingly popular game.

Watchdog of the American People

The SEC has, therefore, gained the importance due it in a society in which the industrial revolution and its consequences of corporate and financial power have occupied such a large part. . . . What has the SEC done?

It has forced the New York Stock Exchange to behave, by liquidating the crooks and by imposing strict rules of conduct which have made subsequent efforts at fraud easier to detect and to limit. Short selling and insiders' manipulations are controlled or forbidden. The New York Stock Exchange itself, even though still a private corporation, is no longer run like a private club. Its governors, moving under the constant glare of the SEC, have become sensitive to the demands of public trust inherent in the activities over which they preside. Operations of the members of the Exchange are closely and continuously watched. . . .

The SEC has, through its enforcement of margin regulations established by the Federal Reserve Board, introduced an element of responsibility and steadiness in stock-market operations. One of the important causes of the 1929 crash was the excessive stock speculation on credit, which made it possible for financially irresponsible individuals, pushed on by stockbrokers, to operate in Wall Street even though often 90 per cent of the money they used was borrowed. . . .

The SEC regulatory procedures have had another, and perhaps unexpected, consequence. They have re-educated the American corporation, the major issuer of new securities, and made it realize that it would be desirable to go even beyond the legal requirements and give to the investor, in plentiful abundance, all kinds of detail about the business whose financial support was to be solicited. Hence, the average prospectus has become a fascinating source of information about the promoters of the industrial venture it describes, their backgrounds and relationships, their interests, the specific outlook of the particular venture, and the general outlook of the industry as a whole. The public's awareness of the nature and of the risks of the private economic process has been much enlarged and the corporations have in yet another way been brought to underline the element of public trust in their activities. . . .

Under the Investment Company Act of 1940 the SEC . . . watches daily and from hour to hour the operations of the stock exchanges. It is not an exaggeration to say that the SEC is acting as the conscience and as the watchdog of the American people in all phases of its financial operations. The pervasive influence of the SEC is easy to notice in the financial world. It dominates the thoughts and the actions of Wall Street. It is the one regulatory commission whose presence is continuously felt in the sphere it regulates. Its powers of exposure, of suspension from trading activities and privileges of both brokers and corporations are so drastic and so feared that they have achieved most of the results that could reasonably have been expected. . . .

A New Financial Morality

It is, of course, quite true that, particularly since the catastrophe of October, 1929, some notable changes have occurred in the operations of the "capitalistic" system and in the behavior of corporations. But in the shower of optimistic words flowing from Wall Street, two things are ignored as a rule. The first is that no one can fully anticipate the ultimate consequences of this multiplication ad infinitum of the numbers of American stockholders. . . .

The second is that, quite apart from their intrinsic nature, these developments have come about largely because their acceptance has been forced on a bewildered financial and economic community by Roosevelt's New Deal. By a psychological transfer not unknown in historical experience, those who most vociferously opposed reform have now come to like it; its obvious advantages have benefited not only the community at large but also those immediately affected by it, the corporations and the purveyors of financial services. Nothing appears simpler than claiming credit for a new economy to which they have contributed little or nothing at all, by comparison with the contributions of the political community acting through Washington.

What matters, however, is: the control the American people now have exercised in an atmosphere of freedom and of private initiative over the vast flow of their financial life; a new financial morality now accepted by an advanced industrial society; and the praise of the regulated themselves for the regulators. A sweeping transfer of economic power, as far as the general setting up of the conditions and procedures under which private activities are to be carried out, has taken place—from Wall Street to Washington. And what should be remembered throughout the so-called capitalistic West is this: the United States still stands alone in having accomplished this task so completely.

Social Security Protects the Elderly and Infirm

Arthur M. Schlesinger Jr.

In late June 1934, President Roosevelt established the Committee of Economic Security, chaired by Secretary of Labor Frances Perkins. (Fifty-one at the time, the intelligent, articulate, highly educated, and hardworking Perkins, a native of Massachusetts, was the country's first female cabinet member.) The committee's task was to formulate a social security program that would provide regular payments for needy people who could not work, primarily those who were elderly or sick, and also needy children. The result was the Social Security Act of 1935, one of the most important and far-reaching federal programs in American history. This summary of the program's inception, passage, and major provisions is from Pulitzer Prize–winning historian Arthur M. Schlesinger's monumental history of the New Deal.

On January 15, 1935, the Committee on Economic Security transmitted its reports to the President. Roosevelt already had his own views on social security. "There is no reason why everybody in the United States should not be covered," he once said to Miss Perkins. "I see no reason why every child, from the day he is born, shouldn't be a member of the social security system. . . . I don't see why not," he continued as Miss Perkins, appalled by the administrative problems of universal coverage, shook her head. "I don't see why not. Cradle to the grave—from the cradle to the grave they ought to be in a social insurance system."

He had in addition specific views about the character of a

Excerpted from *The Coming of the New Deal*, by Arthur M. Schlesinger Jr. Copyright ©1958, renewed 1986 by Arthur M. Schlesinger Jr. Reprinted by permission of Houghton Mifflin Company. All rights reserved.

social insurance program. Thus he believed that public insurance should be built upon the same principles as private insurance. "If I have anything to say about it," he once remarked, "it will always be contributed, and I prefer it to be contributed, both on the part of the employer and the employee, on a sound actuarial basis. It means no money out of the Treasury." This meant a self-supporting system, financed by contributions and special taxes rather than out of the general tax revenue. Frances Perkins, arguing against employee contributions, pointed out that the employer shifted the payroll tax to the consumer in any case, so that employees were already paying their share; [Roosevelt's advisor Rex] Tugwell, arguing against the payroll tax, pointed out that this amounted to a form of sales tax and meant that the system would be financed by those who could least afford it; but none of this argument availed. "I guess you're right on the economics," Roosevelt explained to another complainant some years later, "but those taxes were never a problem of economics. They are politics all the way through. We put those payroll contributions there so as to give the contributors a legal, moral, and political right to collect their pensions and their unemployment benefits. With those taxes in there, no damn politician can ever scrap my social security program."

Borrowing from the Future

On January 17, 1935, Roosevelt sent a message to Congress requesting social security legislation. On the same day [Senator Robert F.] Wagner introduced the draft bill in the Senate and [Congressman David J.] Lewis, jointly with Congressman Robert L. Doughton of North Carolina, introduced it in the House. . . .

The Committee on Economic Security, confronting the problem of the aged, proposed a compulsory system of contributory payments by which workers could build up gradually their rights to annuities in their old age. This left the problem of persons on the verge of retirement who had had no past opportunity to contribute to their own old-age pensions. The best way in which these aging workers could be taken care of, the Committee concluded, was through the federal government's paying a share of the cost. By 1980, according to its estimate, the government would have to contribute to the old-age system around $1.4 billion a year. The Committee conceded that the creation of this commitment would impose a burden on future generations. But the alternative would be to increase reserves at a far higher rate and thus impose a double burden on the present generation, which would have to contribute not only to its own annuities but to the unearned annuities of people middle-aged or over. "The plan we advocate," said the Committee, "amounts to having each generation pay for the support of the people then living who are old."

[Secretary of the Treasury Henry] Morgenthau had accepted the Committee plan and signed the report. Yet as he meditated the financing scheme, he began to feel a certain immorality, as he told the Ways and Means Committee, in the notion of "borrowing from the future to pay the costs." Roosevelt shared Morgenthau's disapproval. "It is almost dishonest," he told Frances Perkins, "to build up an accumulated deficit for the Congress of the United States to meet in 1980. We can't do that. We can't sell the United States short in 1980 any more than in 1935."

Two Proposed Plans Compared

The Treasury alternative was to raise the rates of contribution and thereby build a much larger reserve fund, so that future needs could be met from the fund rather than by levies on current general revenue. This fund, Morgenthau suggested, could be applied to the reduction of the national debt. Roosevelt even supposed that it might eventually serve as the sole customer for federal bonds, thus freeing the government from reliance on private bankers. Under the original plan, the maximum size of the reserve fund would have been less than $12 billion; under the Treasury plan, it would amount to $50 billion by 1980. The Treasury plan had obvious disadvantages. It shifted the burden of providing for currently aging workers from the population as a whole to the younger wage-earners. "Our programs," said Abraham Epstein [an influential advocate of social security], "actually relieve the wealthy from their traditional obligation under the ancient poor laws." Moreover, the creation of so large a fund involved economic risks. As Alvin Hansen on the Technical Board and Marion Folsom of the Eastman Kodak Company on the Advisory Council pointed out, it would divert a large amount of money from consumer purchasing power; "that is bound," Folsom said, "to have a depressing effect on general conditions." And the problem of finding ways to invest $50 billion seemed packed with difficulties.

The self-sustaining theory of social insurance meant in effect that the poor had to pay most of the cost of keeping the poor. Yet, whether because of this or in spite of this, the House Committee quickly adopted the reserve system; probably the idea that private insurance should serve as the model was too compelling. Moreover, there was the political advantage which so impressed Roosevelt. Under the original plan, the old-age insurance system would be at the mercy of each succeeding Congress; while, with a vast reserve fund built up out of contributions, the people were in a sense creating a clear and present equity in their own retirement benefits. The existence of the reserve thus undoubtedly strengthened the system politically. Yet the impact of the reserve on the business cycle—the withdrawal of large sums of money from the spending stream and the reliance on regressive taxation—doubtless added deflationary tendencies which later in the decade weakened the whole nation economically. In time, it appeared that the administration and the Congress had made the wrong decision in 1935.

The Decay and Collapse of Society?

While the friends of social security were arguing out the details of the program, other Americans were regarding the whole idea with consternation, if not with horror. Organized business had long warned against such pernicious notions. "Unemployment insurance cannot be placed on a sound financial basis," said the National Industrial Conference Board; it will facilitate "ultimate socialistic control of life and industry," said the National Association of Manufacturers.

"Industry," observed Alfred Sloan of General Motors, "has every reason to be alarmed at the social, economic and financial implications. . . . The dangers are manifest." It will undermine our national life "by destroying initiative, discouraging thrift, and stifling individual responsibility" (James L.

Frances Perkins Explains How Social Security Works

This is part of one of Secretary of Labor Frances Perkins's 1935 official public statements about the workings of Social Security.

This act establishes unemployment insurance as a substitute for haphazard methods of assistance in periods when men and women willing and able to work are without jobs. It provides for old age pensions . . . for those who have been unable to provide for the years when they no longer can work. It also provides security for dependent and crippled children, mothers, the indigent disabled and the blind. . . . Old-age benefits in the form of monthly payments are to be paid to individuals who have worked and contributed to the insurance fund in direct proportion to the total wages earned by such individuals in the course of their employment. . . . The minimum monthly payment is to be $10, the maximum $85. These payments will begin in the year 1942 and will be to those who have worked and contributed. . . . As an example of the practical operation of the old-age benefit system, consider for a moment a typical young man of thirty-five years of age, and let us compute the benefits which will accrue to him. Assuming that his income will average $100 per month over the period of thirty years until he reaches the age of sixty-five, the benefit payments due him . . . will provide him with $42.50 per month for the remainder of his life. . . . In the event that death occurs prior to the age of sixty-five, $3½% of the total wages earned by him . . . will be returned to his dependents.

Frances Perkins, "The Social Security Act," quoted in William E. Leuchtenburg, ed., *The New Deal: A Documentary History*. New York: Harper and Row, 1968, pp. 81–82.

Donnelly of the Illinois Manufacturers' Association); it begins a pattern which "sooner or later will bring about the inevitable abandonment of private capitalism" (Charles Denby, Jr., of the American Bar Association); "the downfall of Rome started with corn laws, and legislation of that type" (George P. Chandler of the Ohio Chamber of Commerce). With unemployment insurance no one would work; with old-age and survivors insurance no one would save; the result would be moral decay, financial bankruptcy and the collapse of the republic. One after another, business leaders appeared before House and Senate Committees to invest such dismal prophecies with what remained of their authority.

Republicans in the House faithfully reflected the business position. "Never in the history of the world," said Congressman John Taber of New York, "has any measure been brought in here so insidiously designed as to prevent business recovery, to enslave workers, and to prevent any possibility of the employers providing work for the people." "The lash of the dictator will be felt," cried Congressman Daniel Reed. "And twenty-five million free American citizens will for the first time submit themselves to a fingerprint test." Even a respectable Republican like James W. Wadsworth of New York could only see calamity ahead. "This bill opens the door and invites the entrance into the political field," he darkly exclaimed, "of a power so vast, so powerful as to threaten the integrity of our institutions and to pull the pillars of the temple down upon the heads of our descendants." On a crucial test, all Republicans in the House save one voted to recommit the bill to committee. But, in the end, the opposition collapsed; and, fearing reprisal at the polls, most Republicans, after resisting every step along the way, permitted themselves to be recorded in favor of catastrophe. On April 19, the House passed a somewhat revised bill by a vote of 371 to 33.

Passage in the Senate

In the Senate conservatives continued a desultory resistance. Most of the debate in both Houses was over the old-age rather than the unemployment compensation provisions.

Hastings of Delaware, who predicted that the bill might "end the progress of a great country and bring its people to the level of the average European," offered a motion to strike out old-age insurance. Twelve of nineteen Republican senators supported this move. But again, on the final showdown, political prudence triumphed, and the bill passed on June 19, 1935, by a vote of 76 to 6. Difficulties still remained: the Senate had adopted an amendment to exempt employers with industrial pension plans from coverage under the government system. The administration opposed this both as bad in principle and impractical in operation; but argument over this issue delayed Senate-House agreement for seven more weeks until the Senate conferees yielded.

Perhaps out of dissatisfaction with the Labor Department's presentation of the bill, the House, in redrafting, had removed the Social Security Board from the Labor Department and set it up as a separate agency. The Senate restored the Board to Labor; but in conference it was decided to keep it independent. . . .

For chairman, Roosevelt selected John Gilbert Winant, a former governor of New Hampshire. Winant, a tall, earnest, inarticulate man, whose high cheekbones, gaunt features, and unruly black hair gave him a Lincolnian appearance, was a Bull Mooser of 1912 who had kept the Progressive faith. As governor, he had fought for minimum-wage regulation, old-age assistance, and emergency relief; and he had made a strong impression as a member of the Advisory Council of the Committee for Economic Security. Roosevelt, who had known Winant as a fellow governor, liked and trusted him. The other two members of the Board were Arthur Altmeyer and an Arkansas lawyer named Vincent Myles. . . .

A Dedication to the General Welfare

In the next months the Social Security Board swung into action with quiet efficiency. Facing an administrative challenge of staggering complexity, it operated with steady intelligence and competence. No New Deal agency solved such bewildering problems with such self-effacing smoothness. The old-age insurance program went into quick effect; within two years all 48 states passed unemployment compensation laws in response to the federal tax-offset principle; and the programs of categorical assistance gave state governments new resources to deal with their needy citizens. No government bureau ever directly touched the lives of so many millions of Americans—the old, the jobless, the sick, the needy, the blind, the mothers, the children—with so little confusion or complaint. And the overhead costs for this far-flung and extraordinary operation were considerably less than those of private insurance. For this prodigious achievement, founded on millions of records, clerks, and business machines, major credit went to Altmeyer.

For all the defects of the Act, it still meant a tremendous break with the inhibitions of the past. The federal government was at last charged with the obligation to provide its citizens a measure of protection from the hazards and vicissitudes of life. One hundred and ten years earlier, John Quincy Adams had declared that "the great object of the institution of civil government" was "the progressive improvement of the condition of the governed." With the Social Security Act, the constitutional dedication of federal power to the general welfare began a new phase of national history.

Foreign Relations Under the New Deal

Louis M. Hacker

In addition to the country's huge domestic problems and
the numerous programs launched under the New Deal to
remedy them, Roosevelt and his New Dealers had to contend with foreign affairs in a world that grew increasingly
dangerous throughout the 1930s. This comprehensive,
lucid overview of New Deal foreign policy was penned by
former Columbia University scholar Louis M. Hacker. In
addition to the major international events from 1930 to
1941, Hacker covers mutual protection treaties and trade
agreements made between the United States and its Latin
American neighbors, the prevailing isolationist mood in
the United States until the late 1930s, and Roosevelt's
eventual realization that the nation must begin preparing
itself for the likelihood of a global war.

Up to October, 1937—always excepting the Good Neighbor
policy and Secretary of State [Cordell] Hull's reciprocal
trading program—the New Deal's foreign policy had a defi-
nitely nationalistic orientation. Economic revival in the rest
of the world apparently was not to be a direct concern of the
United States; if America could reestablish high levels of
employment and increase its national income, then our
prosperity would flow out beyond our shores and in time
cover the whole earth. That we had become fully integrated
into world affairs politically and economically—and that we
could not pull ourselves up by our own bootstraps—were
ideas only dimly felt in Washington.

An American delegation was sent to London in June,

Excerpted from *Shaping the American Tradition*, by Louis M. Hacker, 1947. Repub-
lished with permission from Columbia University Press, 562 W. 113th St., New
York, NY 10025, via Copyright Clearance Center, Inc.

1933, to attend the World Economic Conference, which was to concern itself with the stabilization of currencies, the freeing of the flow of world trade, and international prices. And then suddenly by Roosevelt's order—and to the dismay of Europeans generally—the Americans refused to tie their currency to that of the British or promise to defend the gold standard. The conference ended in failure.

Congress showed no greater wisdom. In April, 1934, it passed the Johnson Act. Under this, those nations which had received loans from the American government during World War I and which after 1930 had defaulted on interest payments were denied the right to float public securities in the American money market. Thus American capital resources were not to be made available to the European powers for the purposes of assisting them in coming to grips with their own economic difficulties; or indeed in helping them obtain funds here for rearmament purposes after 1936, when the menace of Hitler had become very real.

The Good Neighbor Policy

In our relations with the countries of the Western Hemisphere we were more farsighted. . . . A good beginning had been made by Secretaries of State Kellogg and Stimson during 1927–33. Roosevelt, with the assistance of Secretary of State Cordell Hull, happily continued along these paths. In his First Inaugural, Roosevelt had defined the Good Neighbor as one who "resolutely respects himself, and because he does so, respects the rights of others—the neighbor who respects his obligations and respects the sanctity of his agreements in and with a world of neighbors."

When revolution broke out in Cuba, Roosevelt not only refused to intervene, but he also offered and sent American economic assistance to the distressed republic. In 1934, the new government of Cuba was recognized; and a few months later, our protectorate was terminated by the repeal of the Platt Amendment. The same summer saw the recall of American marines from Haiti; and in 1935, the United States relinquished its financial control over the Haitian government. Also in 1935, cooperating with Latin American governments, the United States succeeded in terminating the war between Chile and Paraguay; and in 1936 our treaty rights in Panama were given up and that little republic was now truly independent for the first time.

In January, 1936, Roosevelt appeared in person at the Pan American conference being held at Buenos Aires—he was the first President of the United States ever to have visited South America while in office—and gave further pledges of his devotion to the idea of the Good Neighbor. A consultative pact was signed under which the signatories pledged to consult together in the event of war or intervention in the Western Hemisphere. The United States was moving toward converting the Good Neighbor policy into a multilateral understanding.

This, in fact, was achieved in 1940 at the Havana Conference when the so-called Act of Havana was drawn up. The Act of Havana was prefaced by the statement that "the status of regions in this continent belonging to European Powers is a subject of deep concern to all the governments of the American Republics." And then the Act went on to pledge all the signatories to regard as an aggressive measure against all of them "any attempt on the part of a non-American State against the integrity or inviolability of the territory, the sovereignty, or the political independence of an American State." It is true that the Monroe Doctrine [which forbade outside powers from interfering in American affairs and territory] continued to be stated as an American unilateral declaration; but the Act of Havana reaffirmed it in multilateral terms. To this degree, therefore, the Latin American nations were prepared to accept the pledge of the United States that the Monroe Doctrine was directed against non-American Powers entirely.

Trade Agreements

The Reciprocal Trade Agreements Act of 1934 gave the President power to conclude with other countries conventions under which tariff rates could be reduced as much as 50 percent—all this without the need for calling upon Congress to approve. There was only one safeguard included in the act: no item was to be added to or taken from the free list. Under the law, the State Department was to draw up the agreements, being assisted in these activities by a series of interdepartmental committees headed by experts. Public hearings were to be held, in order to afford proper protection for the interests of American business groups. The most-favored nation idea was also provided for, so that concessions granted to one country would apply to all countries that did not discriminate against us. Thus the benefits of revision downward would spread out in widening circles, including not only those nations which signed agreements with us but also those nations with whom signatories of the American acts were writing new agreements.

By 1937, when the act was renewed for another three years, agreements had already been written with fourteen countries. These covered more than a third of our total foreign trade, and they had the effect of increasing foreign trade with the signatory nations more than 40 percent. America's tariff wall was still high; but, at least, we were showing good faith in our desire to break down barriers to free exchanges the world over. Congress continued to renew the Trade Agreements Act in the 1930s and 1940s.

The Neutrality Acts

Despite these manifestations of an interest in the world outside our shores, the prevailing American temper was isolationist. Nothing demonstrated this better than the Neutrality Acts of 1935, 1936, and 1937. As a result of the investigations of the Senate Munitions Committee, headed by Gerald P. Nye of North Dakota, Congress and a good part of the American people had become convinced that the munition makers had in very considerable measure been responsible for the entrance of the United States into World War I. To prevent our involvement in new international conflicts, therefore, Congress passed the first of its Neutrality Laws in August, 1935. This provided that upon the outbreak of war, an embargo was to be imposed by the President upon the export of implements of war; also, at his discretion, he might prohibit Americans from traveling on the ships of belligerent nations except at their own risk. The act was to be in force until February, 1936.

The second Neutrality Act—the joint resolution of February, 1936, which was to apply until May, 1937—further cut down the area of presidential discretionary action. In 1935, Italy had invaded Ethiopia, and Americans saw the League of Nations struggling ineffectively against this act of aggression. They were sure, therefore, they were on the right course; we must not be drawn into the troubles of Europe at any price. The second act, therefore, preserved the mandatory embargo on implements of war and permitted the President to extend it to other exports. Belligerent powers were to be denied the right to raise funds in American money markets.

Between the second and the third neutrality acts, civil war broke out in Spain; Italy, Germany, and Russia intervened; and the Berlin-Rome Axis was established. There was no doubt that an international conflict was impending. In such a climate, with the isolationists still in the saddle, the third Neutrality Act—the joint resolution of May 1, 1937—was drawn up. Unlike its predecessors, this was to be a permanent commitment. It continued the mandatory embargo on arms, munitions, and implements of war and the prohibition on credits to belligerents. It denied Americans the right to travel on ships of belligerents under any circumstances. It refused to allow American merchant ships to arm. And, for two years, all goods destined for nations at war were to come under the "cash and carry" provision: they were to be carried away in non-American ships and they were to be paid for before they left the country.

The Flames of War

Up to this time, Roosevelt's own attitude toward the disorders beginning to appear throughout the world remained unclear. So, in January, 1936, he was prepared to accept all the terms of the first Neutrality Act. Again, to the chagrin of many American liberals, it was the President himself who asked Congress in January, 1937, to impose an arms embargo on Spain—and this despite the fact that the duly constituted Loyalist government was being fought by insurgents openly supported by Italy and Germany. Further, in order to apply the arms embargo to the Italo-Ethiopian conflict, the President had declared a state of war in existence before diplomatic relations between the two countries had even been suspended. And on the other hand, he had refused to recognize a state of war in China, even after Japanese aggression had become unmasked, as early as 1931.

By 1936, it was apparent that Japan was ready to cut herself free from all international commitments. In January of that year, the Japanese delegation quit the naval conference in London because the other Powers would not grant Japan parity; this meant the denunciation of the London Naval Treaty of 1930 and the resumption of capital ship construction. And in November, Japan signed the Anti-Comintern Pact: it had taken its stand beside the other two aggressors, Germany and Italy.

In July, 1937, the Japanese launched their full-scale offensive against the Chinese. . . . Before the year was over, without the formal declaration of war, Japan had extended its military operations over a good part of northern and central China. The Japanese poured armies into that unhappy country and engaged in atrocities against civilian populations.

One such was the general aerial bombing of the populous city of Nanking. It was after this attack that President Roosevelt came to understand that America no longer could remain an onlooker as the flames of war crept over the world. In Chicago on October 5, he delivered his famous Quarantine Address in which he called the attention of the American people to the fact that Japanese, German, and Italian aggression was imperilling our safety. And he issued this portentous warning to his fellow countrymen:

> Let no one imagine that America will escape, that America may expect mercy, that this Western Hemisphere will not be attacked and that it will continue tranquilly and peacefully to carry on the ethics and the arts of civilization. . . . If we are to have a world in which we can breathe freely and live in amity without fear, the peace-loving nations must make a concerted effort to uphold laws and principles on which peace can rest secure. . . .

President Roosevelt declared boldly, therefore, that he would quarantine aggressors. From that day to the attack on Pearl Harbor, the administration left no stone unturned to prepare the United States against future eventualities.

Putting America's House in Order

In January, 1938, the President called Congress' attention to the fact that other nations were rearming; and he asked for new naval construction. Congress quickly complied and passed the administration measure much as the naval experts had drawn it up. The Naval Act of 1938 authorized the expenditure of more than a billion dollars on new capital ships, airplane carriers, and cruisers; the United States was beginning to move toward the development of that two-ocean navy which alone could defend the two seas on which it faced.

Meanwhile, relations with Japan were steadily deteriorating. In December, 1937, Japanese aircraft bombed and destroyed the American gunboat *Panay* on the Yangtsze River. It is true that the Japanese made immediate apologies and offered indemnification; but the State Department refused to assume that this was to be the last of the unfriendly acts of the Japanese toward the United States.

Checking Japanese aggression was not an easy matter, however. And America's position was becoming increasingly difficult as the European Powers themselves found no formulas to preserve peace. In September, 1938, England and France abandoned Czechoslovakia to its fate when they surrendered the Sudetenland to Hitler at Munich. In March, 1939, Hitler marched into Czechoslovakia with none to gainsay him; in the same month he took Memel. In April, Mussolini seized Albania. France and England knew that Poland was to be the next victim, and they declared unequivocally that they would fight if Hitler moved eastward. But Hitler was wiser than they assumed; he was not ready—yet—to wage a two-front war. He proceeded to assure his safety on the east by the German-Soviet Pact of August 22, 1939. On September 1, the German armies were in Poland and World War II had commenced.

Poland quickly fell while the French army sat behind the

safety—so it believed—of the Maginot Line. And then, after they had exploited fully the psychological effects of the so-called "phony war" in the west, the German armies swung across the Rhine into the Low Countries and France. France, unprepared and badly led, fell in June, 1940. Only England stood out against the successful German Wehrmacht [air force]. And in September, 1940, Japan, Germany, and Italy signed the Tripartite Pact, which bound them together in a military alliance.

Only now did America begin to put its house in order. The navy was granted further appropriations; the President was given the right to call out the National Guard; in September, the Selective Service Act was passed. To protect us from surprise attacks—and to help England—in the same month we released fifty overage destroyers to the British navy in exchange for long-term leases in British possessions in the Western Hemisphere where we could build air and naval bases. Our vigilance toward the Japanese also was commendable. In July, 1940—to check the flow of vital war materials eastward—the Export Control Act gave the President power to curtail or prohibit the movement of such goods. Licenses were refused for the export of aviation gasoline and most types of machine tools. In October, the export of iron and steel scrap to Japan was embargoed.

Then, we committed ourselves. For, in March, 1941, Congress passed the Lend-Lease Act—and we were launched, as Roosevelt said, upon a "policy of unqualified, immediate, all-out aid for Britain, Greece, China, and for all the governments in exile whose homelands are temporarily occupied by the aggressors." An undeclared naval war broke out in the Atlantic; but Japan and not Hitler struck first.

One World

On June 22, 1941, without warning, Germany attacked Russia; and at the same time Japanese pretensions toward the whole of southeastern Asia were revealed. It was evident to America that Japan was preparing for a large-scale offensive that threatened not only French Indo-China (which indeed it had already occupied), but also Malaya, Burma, and the

Netherlands Indies. We warned the Japanese against such moves; and for a time they temporized. They sent a new ambassador, Admiral Nomura, to Washington and he and Secretary Hull carried on discussions during the greater part of 1941. In November, Nomura was joined by a special emissary, Saburo Kurusu; there were further conversations, with Roosevelt and Hull both participating in them—but no agreements were reached. Meanwhile General Tojo, an open warmonger, had become the Japanese prime minister; and it was plain to American Ambassador Grew at Tokyo that Japan meant to fight. Washington was warned accordingly, and members of the administration, in public addresses, began to prepare the American people for hostilities.

The attack came from an unexpected quarter. Early Sunday morning, December 7, the Japanese struck at Pearl Harbor from the air. The next day, President Roosevelt appeared before Congress and asked for the declaration of a state of war. Congress complied at once, there being but one dissenting vote. Three days later, Germany and Italy declared war on the United States.

The United States was in World War II. It was committed to the destruction of the Axis Powers and to the termination of the threat of aggression everywhere. After more than twenty years, America had returned to take its place in that "one world" which it had mistakenly assumed it could disregard. American prosperity and security were linked with welfare and peace everywhere on the face of the earth. To this point the Third American Revolution [Roosevelt's New Deal] had brought the American people, some three and one-half centuries after Elizabethan England had begun to dream of establishing settlements on the North American mainland.

Roosevelt and the New Deal at Odds with the Supreme Court

Paul K. Conkin

Some of Roosevelt's critics thought that he and his administration wielded too much power and that a number of his New Deal programs were too radical or even of dubious legality. To some degree the Supreme Court eventually agreed. On May 27, 1935, it declared the National Industrial Recovery Act (NIRA) unconstitutional, and in 1936 it struck down the processing tax levied by the Agricultural Adjustment Act, robbing the government of sorely needed revenue. In the following essay, University of Wisconsin scholar Paul K. Conkin tells how these events angered President Roosevelt to the point that he decided to attempt to pack the Court with his own appointees. The result, says Conkin, was that the administration, and by association the New Deal, suffered a serious loss of prestige and authority.

In 1936 Roosevelt clearly had the support of a large majority of the people. When they voted for him, they presumably also voted for the New Deal and its continuation. Sixty percent approved, whatever their degree of understanding. They confirmed Roosevelt's own sense of righteousness and confirmed his distaste for his more vocal critics. Yet already the courts had nullified much New Deal legislation. And by 1935 Congress was becoming restless and increasingly concerned about the power it had surrendered in a time of crisis. Key sections of the NIRA [National Industrial Recovery Act] and the Agricultural Adjustment Act fell before the courts, while a Congress susceptible to lobbying influences had dwarfed a

Excerpted from *The New Deal*, 2nd ed., by Paul K. Conkin. Copyright 1975 by Harlan Davidson, Inc., pp. 87–91. Reprinted by permission.

major tax bill and, on a test vote forced by Roosevelt, had weakened the utilities bill. Roosevelt detested such flagrant defiance of the majority's will and of his own will. A man who usually had his way, and now seemed worthy of it by democratic choice and moral right, fought back. As a democrat, he refused to acquiesce in the institutional barriers that often nullified the will of the majority or even to fight back by means legitimized by these same institutions.

The Controversial Court Bill

The United States claims to be both a democracy, in which the will of the people is supreme, and a constitutional republic, or a government of law, in which established principles prevail over the whim of a majority or the assertions of a popular leader. Abstractly conceived, the conflict between the two is complete. In American practice the conflict has usually been muted. Not in the New Deal. Roosevelt, burdened to carry out the will of the people, angered at threats to his own power and good intentions, tried to remove the impediment of law. By suggesting that Congress give him, in effect, the power to bring the Supreme Court into line with administrative policies, he moved toward a more complete democracy, or a government more directly responsive to the will of the majority. In a decade of propaganda, of highly emotional and irrational political movements, of charismatic leaders, this proposed shift in government aroused opposition from all sides and most fervently from civil libertarians.

The Court Bill of 1937 was ostensibly a reform measure. In fact, it was a perfectly transparent instrument for permitting Roosevelt to make enough extra, pro–New Deal appointments to the Supreme Court to alter the close decisions on New Deal legislation. The device was a provision allowing extra appointments for unretired judges over the age of seventy. Roosevelt plotted the bill in secrecy, sprung it by complete surprise on Congress, defended it by hypocritical arguments, and then pushed it by every political trick, every type of ruthless pressure and cunning he possessed. The central issue was not the constitutionality of New Deal measures, or the incapacity of the existing Court.

It had been quite vigorous in its frequent dissent but also continuously divided. At issue was an institutional arrangement, in part rooted in the Constitution, in part a product of tradition. The Supreme Court early gained the right of constitutional review, or the power to nullify acts of Congress on appeal of aggrieved litigants. It could do this when, in its judgment, such acts violated the terms of the Constitution, the highest and most stable expression of popular will.

The Limits of Presidential Power

Just as much as Roosevelt, the Supreme Court judges represented power, not drawn as directly from the people but nonetheless anchored in the public acceptance of constitutionalism and of appointed, life-tenured judges to interpret the Constitution. The Court issue also gave the concealed opponents of Roosevelt a made-to-order opportunity to switch sides or vent previously unvoiced grievances. Thus the Court battle was a struggle in power politics as well as in grand principles of government. The Court won and Roosevelt lost. But only after a long, agonizing congressional session, during which one judge retired and the switch of one vote in a crucial decision (often falsely viewed as a political move by the Court) changed the whole obstructionist profile of the Court and initiated a permanent change toward broader economic regulation.

Just as Roosevelt found the limits of his power in the Court fight, so the Supreme Court probed its limits in the thirties. The Supreme Court, as the president, had a limited amount of power. Back of both, back of a balanced system of government, were the beliefs and habits of a people. Law, particularly constitutional law, exists as a stabilizing, restraining influence on popular government, equally preserving entrenched privilege and preventing new tyranny, particularly that dressed in the popular fashion of the mob. But Court restraints cannot permanently impede something desired by a vast majority. Fortunately, the amendment process provides a technique, although a difficult technique, for achieving change, as does the more informal process of changing interpretation. Roosevelt wanted a quicker answer

and believed he had enough support to secure it. By impli-
cation, he wanted to politicize the Court so as to secure a
constitution that could, like the English, be amended by leg-

---

The Court Declares the NIRA Unconstitutional

*This May 27, 1935, AP news release announces the ruling made by
the Supreme Court that day, striking down the National Industrial
Recovery Act (and by default, the National Recovery Administration,
or NRA, the agency that ran the NIRA).*

The administration bowed tonight before a Supreme Court
ruling that reduced the NRA to a scrap of paper, announcing
that all measures for compulsory enforcement of codes had
been abandoned, but pleading for a continued code observance.

Apparently fearful of a return to unbridled competitive conditions, following a unanimous verdict of unconstitutionality from
the high court, Donald R. Richberg, NRA head, discussed future
steps with President Roosevelt and decided upon the two actions.

On two specific counts, the court found the sections of the
National Industrial Recovery Act unconstitutional.

It held that Congress had illegally delegated its own powers
to the president in authorizing him to approve and promulgate
the codes.

It ruled that Congress may not reach into a community and
tell a poultry dealer whose business only indirectly affects interstate commerce how much he shall pay his help and what the
latter's working hours shall be.

The verdict of the court threw the administration and Congress into a state of confusion and bewilderment.

So sweeping was it, that it left them groping for means of
creating a new NRA on the wreckage of the old, and posed to
them the question of whether that could be done without more
legal dispute.

In addition to the all-important question of what now shall
become of NRA, the decision at once set New Dealers to pondering the constitutionality of other key measures—the codes
of AAA, federal control of the liquor industry, and the Wagner
labor disputes act.

islative action instead of the more cumbersome American practice of having the people act in a special constitutional capacity. He also wanted to restrict the nonelective legisla-

Labor was disappointed, too. William Green, president of the AFL, hastened back to Washington from New York, and Francis J. Gorman, vice president of the United Textile Workers, warned that departures from the textile code's wage and hours provisions would be followed by immediate strikes. . . .

"We face now the question of maintaining the gains which have been made in the last two years and retaining the values which have been created under the National Recovery Administration," Richberg said.

"It seems clear that that question must be decided by the administration and the Congress and the people of the United States within a very short time."

The high court's decision, read by Chief Justice Charles Evans Hughes before a tense courtroom into which crowded Richberg and other New Deal lights, stirred the capital as has nothing else for months.

Reading slowly and with emphasis, Chief Justice Hughes marked out the two main counts against the NRA. At one point he said:

"Extraordinary conditions may call for extraordinary remedies, but the argument stops short of attempting to defend action outside of constitutional authority.

"Extraordinary conditions do not create constitutional power."

Spreading out from Hughes' words were a swift rush of developments, statements of opinion and of ideas as to what should be done to handle the situation. . . .

The opinion of the seven, prepared and delivered by Chief Justice Hughes, was emphatic in its assertions the law delegated congressional powers to the president without sufficient restrictions and limitations to bring that action inside the scope of the Constitution.

Quoted in Associated Press Writers, *The Great Depression, 1929–1939.* Danbury, CT: Grolier, 1995, pp. 158–59.

tive power disguised in the right of constitutional review. Felix Frankfurter, a major adviser and in the tradition of [noted Court Justice] Oliver W. Holmes, also believed that the courts should not lightly challenge legislative will, and never if they could find any interpretative leeway.

Why the Court Overturned Some New Deal Legislation

The sharply divided Supreme Court of the thirties did not represent clear juristic theories. As yet, no historian has seriously studied the Court fight. Much the pity, for here was probably the most important issue to arise in the New Deal. The important cases show no clear pattern, except a near unanimity of opposition to expansion of federal power by four judges, a willingness to support most Roosevelt policies by three judges, and a general willingness by all judges to wade boldly into the constitutional issues raised by the legislative flood. Like the Warren Court later, the judges rejected a narrow doctrine of judicial restraint. Or, like Roosevelt, they did not hesitate to use the power they possessed. They overturned New Deal legislation for several reasons— undue delegation of legislative power, overextension of the commerce clause, denial of due process and of contract rights, and, in one important state case on minimum wages, because of a balancing of technical issues rather than a substantive issue. The Court was most atavistic [adhering to older, traditional principles] in its narrow interpretation of interstate commerce and thus in limiting the range of federal economic regulation; most prophetic in censoring new administrative procedures on libertarian grounds, and, often led by the so-called conservative foursome in unheralded cases, in strictly upholding the rights of free speech and press.

The Court fight wasted a congressional session, helped destroy the Roosevelt myth of invincibility, disillusioned many of his former disciples, divided the Democratic party, gave the Republican party a new lease on life, and left Roosevelt bitter and hurt. As always, he became deeply involved in the battle and scarcely remembered what was at issue. In his frustration he exhibited his worst and most militant character traits and thus further aided his opponents. But there was partial redemption for Roosevelt. Some of his most bitter enemies came out even worse. Their onslaught of cheap propaganda, including shabby tricks, outright lies, and fantastic charges, made Roosevelt look like a gentleman.

After the New Deal

Turning | Points
IN WORLD HISTORY

The Legacy of the Depression and the New Deal

William E. Leuchtenburg

William E. Leuchtenburg, a recognized authority on the depression era, provides this summary of the accomplishments and legacy of Roosevelt's New Deal programs. Leuchtenburg begins by citing the various common criticisms of the New Deal leveled by later scholars and politicians, suggesting that, overall, Roosevelt's efforts failed to halt the depression and even proved harmful by creating a permanent welfare state. Leuchtenburg finds certain aspects of these arguments valid and admits that the New Deal was certainly no panacea. But he goes on to point out that it was still an incredible achievement, one unmatched in scope and sheer creativity to this day. All things considered, Leuchtenburg finds the New Deal a huge and courageous, if imperfect, social experiment that permanently altered American life in a great many positive ways.

The fiftieth anniversary of the New Deal, launched on March 4, 1933, comes at a time when it has been going altogether out of fashion. Writers on the left, convinced that the Roosevelt experiment was either worthless or pernicious, have assigned it to the dustbin of history. Commentators on the right, though far less conspicuous, see in the New Deal the origins of the centralized state they seek to dismantle. . . .

To be sure, the New Deal has always had its critics. In Roosevelt's own day Marxists said that the New Deal had not done anything for agriculture that an earthquake could not have done better at the same time that conservatives were saying that FDR was unprincipled. Hoover even called

Excerpted from William E. Leuchtenburg, "The Achievement of the New Deal," in *Fifty Years Later: The New Deal Evaluated*, edited by Harvard Sitkoff (New York: Knopf, 1985). Reprinted by permission of the author.

him "a chameleon on plaid." Most historians have long since accepted the fact that New Deal policies were sometimes inconsistent, that Roosevelt failed to grasp countercyclical fiscal theory, that recovery did not come until armaments orders fueled the economy, that the President was credited with certain reforms like insurance of bank deposits that he, in fact, opposed, that a number of New Deal programs, notably aid for the marginal farmer, were inadequately financed, and that some New Deal agencies discriminated against blacks.

During the 1960s historians not only dressed up these objections as though they were new revelations but carried their disappointment with contemporary liberalism to the point of arguing either that the New Deal was not just inadequate but actually malign [harmful] or that the New Deal was so negligible as to constitute a meaningless episode. . . . The New Deal was now perceived to be elitist, since it had neglected to consult the poor about what legislation they wanted, or to encourage the participation of ghetto-dwellers in decision-making. Roosevelt's policies, historians maintained, redounded to the benefit of those who already had advantages—wealthier staple farmers, organized workers, business corporations, the "deserving poor"—while displacing sharecroppers and neglecting the powerless. An "antirevolutionary response to a situation that had revolutionary potentialities," the New Deal, it was said, missed opportunities to nationalize the banks and restructure the social order. Even "providing assistance to the needy and . . . rescuing them from starvation" served conservative ends, historians complained, for these efforts "sapped organized radicalism of its waning strength and of its potential constituency among the unorganized and discontented." The Roosevelt Administration, it has been asserted, failed to achieve more than it did not as a result of the strength of conservative opposition but because of the intellectual deficiencies of the New Dealers and because Roosevelt deliberately sought to save "large-scale corporate capitalism." In *Towards a New Past*, the New Left historian Barton Bernstein summed up this point of view: "The New Deal failed to solve the problem of depression, it failed to raise the impoverished, it failed to redistribute income, it failed to extend equality and generally countenanced racial discrimination and segregation."

Although the characterization of Bernstein as "New Left" suggests that he represents a deviant persuasion, the New Left perspective has, in fact, all but become the new orthodoxy, even though there is not yet any New Left survey of the domestic history of the United States in the 1930s. This emphasis has so permeated writing on the New Deal in the past generation that an instructor who wishes to assign the latest thought on the age of Roosevelt has a wide choice of articles and anthologies that document the errors of the New Deal but no assessment of recent vintage that explores its accomplishments.

The fiftieth anniversary of the New Deal provides the occasion for a modest proposal—that we reintroduce some tension into the argument over the interpretation of the Roosevelt years. If historians are to develop a credible synthesis, it is important to regain a sense of the achievement of the New Deal. . . . As a first step toward a more considered evaluation, one has to remind one's self not only of what the New Deal did not do, but of what it achieved.

New Deal Changes

Above all, one needs to recognize how markedly the New Deal altered the character of the State in America. Indeed, though for decades past European theorists had been talking about *der Staat*, there can hardly be said to have been a State in America in the full meaning of the term before the New Deal. If you had walked into an American town in 1932, you would have had a hard time detecting any sign of a federal presence, save perhaps for the post office and even many of today's post offices date from the 1930s. Washington rarely affected people's lives directly. There was no national old-age pension system, no federal unemployment compensation, no aid to dependent children, no federal housing, no regulation of the stock market, no withholding tax, no federal school lunch, no farm subsidy, no national minimum wage law, no welfare state. As late as Herbert Hoover's presidency, it was regarded as axiomatic [self-evident] that government activity should be minimal. In the pre-Roosevelt era, even organized labor and the National Conference of Social Workers opposed federal action on behalf of the unemployed. The New Deal sharply challenged these shibboleths [common beliefs]. From 1933 to 1938, the government intervened in a myriad of ways from energizing the economy to fostering unionization. . . .

Although the New Deal always operated within a capitalist matrix and the government sought to enhance profitmaking, Roosevelt and his lieutenants rejected the traditional view that government was the handmaiden of business or that government and business were coequal sovereigns. As a consequence, they adopted measures to discipline corporations, to require a sharing of authority with government and unions, and to hold businessmen accountable. In the early days of the National Recovery Administration (NRA), the novelist Sherwood Anderson wrote:

> I went to several code hearings. No one has quite got their significance. Here for the first time you see these men of business, little ones and big ones, . . . coming up on the platform to give an accounting. It does seem the death knell of the old idea that a man owning a factory, office or store has a right to run it in his own way.
>
> There is at least an effort to relate it now to the whole thing, man's relations with his fellow men etc. Of course it is crude and there will be no end to crookedness, objections, etc. but I do think an entire new principle in American life is being established.

Through a series of edicts and statutes, the administration invaded the realm of the banker by establishing control over the nation's money supply. The government clamped an embargo on gold, took the United States off the gold standard, and nullified the requirement for the payment of gold in private contracts. In 1935 a resentful Supreme Court sustained this authority, although a dissenting justice said that this was Nero at his worst. The Glass-Steagall Banking Act (1933) stripped commercial banks of the privilege of engaging in investment banking, and established federal insurance of bank deposits, an innovation which the leading monetary historians have called "the structural change most conducive to monetary stability since bank notes were taxed out of existence immediately after the Civil War." The Banking Act of 1935 gave the United States what other industrial nations had long had, but America lacked—central banking. This series of changes transformed the relationship between the government and the financial community. . . . As Charles Beard observed: "Having lost their gold coins and bullion to the Federal Government and having filled their vaults with federal bonds and other paper, bankers have become in a large measure mere agents of the Government in Washington. No longer do these powerful interests stand, so to speak, 'outside the Government' and in a position to control or dictate to it."

From the Private to Public Orbit

A number of other enactments helped transfer authority from Wall Street to Washington. The Securities Act of 1933 established government supervision of the issue of securities, and made company directors civilly and criminally liable for misinformation on the statements they were required to file with each new issue. The Securities and Exchange Act of 1934 initiated federal supervision of the stock exchanges, which to this day operate under the lens of the Securities and Exchange Commission (SEC). The Holding Company Act of 1935 levelled some of the utility pyramids, dissolving all utility holding companies that were more than twice removed from their operating companies, and increased the regulatory powers of the SEC over public utilities. . . . To be sure, financiers continued to make important policy choices, but they never again operated in the uninhibited universe of the Great Bull Market. By the spring of 1934, one writer was already reporting:

> Financial news no longer originates in Wall Street. . . . News of a financial nature in Wall Street now is merely an echo of events which take place in Washington. . . . The pace of the ticker is determined now in Washington not in company

boardrooms or in brokerage offices. . . . In Wall Street it is no longer asked what some big trader is doing, what some important banker thinks, what opinion some eminent lawyer holds about some pressing question of the day. The query in Wall Street has become: "What's the news from Washington?"

The age of Roosevelt focused attention on Washington, too, by initiatives in fields that had been regarded as exclusively within the private orbit, notably in housing. The Home Owners' Loan Corporation, created in 1933, saved tens of thousands of homes from foreclosure by refinancing mortgages. In 1934 the Federal Housing Administration (FHA) began its program of insuring loans for the construction and renovation of private homes, and over the next generation more than 10 million FHA-financed units were built. Before the New Deal, the national government had never engaged in public housing, except for the World War I emergency, but agencies like the Public Works Administration now broke precedent. The Tennessee Valley Authority (TVA) laid out the model town of Norris, the Federal Emergency Relief Administration (FERA) experimented with subsistence homesteads, and the Resettlement Administration created greenbelt communities, entirely new towns girdled by green countryside. When in 1937 the Wagner-Steagall Act created the U.S. Housing Authority, it assured public housing a permanent place in American life.

A New Deal for the Common Man

The New Deal profoundly altered industrial relations by throwing the weight of government behind efforts to unionize workers. At the outset of the Great Depression, the American labor movement was "an anachronism in the world," for only a tiny minority of factory workers were unionized. Employers hired and fired and imposed punishments at will, used thugs as strikebreakers and private police, stockpiled industrial munitions, and ran company towns as feudal fiefs. In an astonishingly short period in the Roosevelt years a very different pattern emerged. Under the umbrella of Section 7(a) of the National Industrial Recovery Act of 1933 and of the far-reaching Wagner Act of 1935, union organizers gained millions of recruits in such open-shop strongholds as steel, automobiles, and textiles. Employees won wage rises, reductions in hours, greater job security, freedom from the tyranny of company guards, and protection against arbitrary punishment. Thanks to the National Recovery Administration and the Guffey acts, coal miners achieved the outlawing of compulsory company houses and stores. Steel workers, who in 1920 labored twelve-hour shifts seven days a week at the blast furnaces, were to become so powerful that in the postwar era they would win not merely paid vacations but sabbatical leaves. A British analyst has concluded: "From one of the most restrictive among industrially advanced nations, the labour code of the United States (insofar as it could be said to exist before 1933) was rapidly transformed into one of the most liberal," and these reforms, he adds, "were not the harvest of long-sustained agitation by trade unions, but were forced upon a partly sceptical labor movement by a government which led or carried it into maturity."

Years later, when David E. Lilienthal, the director of the Tennessee Valley Authority, was being driven to the airport to fly to Roosevelt's funeral, the TVA driver said to him:

> I won't forget what he did for me. . . . I spent the best years of my life working at the Appalachian Mills . . . and they didn't even treat us like humans. If you didn't do like they said, they always told you there was someone else to take your job. I had my mother and my sister to take care of. Sixteen cents an hour was what we got; a fellow can't live on that, and you had to get production even to get that, this Bedaux system; some fellows only got twelve cents. If you asked to get off on a Sunday, the foreman would say, "All right you stay away Sunday, but when you come back Monday someone else will have your job." No, sir, I won't forget what he done for us. . . .

The NRA wiped out sweatshops, and removed some 150,000 child laborers from factories. The Walsh-Healey Act of 1936 and the Fair Labor Standards Act of 1938 established the principle of a federally imposed minimal level of working conditions, and added further sanctions against child labor. If the New Deal did not do enough for the "one-third of a nation" to whom Roosevelt called attention, it at least made a beginning, through agencies like the Farm Security Administration, toward helping sharecroppers, tenant farmers, and migrants like John Steinbeck's Joads [in his novel *The Grapes of Wrath*]. Most important, it originated a new system of social rights to replace the dependence on private charity. The Social Security Act of 1935 created America's first national system of old-age pensions and initiated a federal-state program of unemployment insurance. It also authorized grants for the blind, for the incapacitated, and for dependent children, a feature that would have unimaginable long-range consequences. . . .

Roosevelt himself affirmed the newly assumed attitudes in Washington in his annual message to Congress in 1938 when he declared: "Government has a final responsibility for the well-being of its citizenship. If private co-operative endeavor fails to provide work for willing hands and relief for the unfortunate, those suffering hardship from no fault of their own have a right to call upon the Government for aid; and a government worthy of its name must make fitting response."

A New Deal for the Unemployed

Nothing revealed this approach so well as the New Deal's attention to the plight of the millions of unemployed. During the ten years between 1929 and 1939, one scholar has written, "more progress was made in public welfare and relief than in the three hundred years after this country was first settled." A series of alphabet agencies—the FERA, the CWA (Civil Works Administration), the WPA (Works Progress Administration)—provided government work for the jobless, while the National Youth Administration (NYA) employed college students in museums, libraries, and laboratories, enabled high school students to remain in school, and set up a program of apprentice training. In Texas, the twenty-seven-year-old NYA director Lyndon Johnson put penniless young men like John Connally to work building roadside parks, and in North Carolina, the NYA employed, at 35 cents an hour, a Duke University law student, Richard Nixon.

In an address in Los Angeles in 1936, the head of FDR's relief operations, [leading New Dealer] Harry Hopkins, conveyed the attitude of the New Deal toward those who were down and out:

> I am getting sick and tired of these people on the W.P.A. and local relief rolls being called chiselers and cheats. . . . These people . . . are just like the rest of us. They don't drink any more than us, they don't lie any more, they're no lazier than the rest of us—they're pretty much a cross section of the American people. . . . I have never believed that with our capitalistic system people have to be poor. I think it is an outrage that we should permit hundreds and hundreds of thousands of people to be ill clad, to live in miserable homes, not to have enough to eat; not to be able to send their children to school for the only reason that they are poor. I don't believe ever again in America we are going to permit the things to happen that have happened in the past to people. We are never going back . . . to the days of putting the old people in the alms houses, when a decent dignified pension at home will keep them there. We are coming to the day when we are going to have decent houses for the poor, when there is genuine and real security for everybody. I have gone all over the moral hurdles that people are poor because they are bad. I don't believe it. A system of government on that basis is fallacious.

Under the leadership of men like Hopkins, "Santa Claus incomparable and privy-builder without peer," projects of relief agencies and of the Public Works Administration (PWA) changed the face of the land. The PWA built thoroughfares like the Skyline Drive in Virginia and the Overseas Highway from Miami to Key West, constructed the Medical Center in Jersey City, burrowed Chicago's new subway, and gave Natchez, Mississippi, a new bridge, and Denver a modern water-supply system. Few New Yorkers today realize the long reach of the New Deal. If they cross the Triborough Bridge, they are driving on a bridge the PWA built. If they fly into La Guardia Airport, they are landing at an airfield laid out by the WPA. If they get caught in a traffic jam on the FDR Drive, they are using yet another artery built by the WPA.

Even the animal cages in the Central Park Zoo were reconstructed by WPA workers. In New York City, the WPA built or renovated hundreds of school buildings; gave Orchard Beach a bathhouse, a mall, and a lagoon; landscaped Bryant Park and the campus of Hunter College in the Bronx; conducted examinations for venereal disease, filled teeth, operated pollen count stations, and performed puppet shows for disturbed children; it built dioramas for the Brooklyn Museum; ran street dances in Harlem and an open-air night club in Central Park; and, by combing neglected archives, turned up forgotten documents like the court proceedings in the Aaron Burr libel case and the marriage license issued to Captain Kidd. In New York City alone the WPA employed more people than the entire War Department.

Though much of the makework inevitably concentrated on operations like road building, the Roosevelt government proved ingenious in devising other activities. Years later, John Steinbeck recalled:

> When W.P.A. came, we were delighted, because it offered work. . . . I was given the project of taking a census of all the dogs on the Monterey Peninsula, their breeds, weight and characters. I did it very thoroughly and, since I knew my reports were not likely to get to the hands of the mighty, I wrote some pretty searching character studies of poodles, and beagles and hounds. If such records were kept, somewhere in Washington, there will be a complete dog record of the Monterey Peninsula in the early Thirties.

Aid for Artists, Writers, and Filmmakers

The New Deal showed unusual sensitivity toward jobless white-collar workers, notably those in aesthetic fields. The Public Works of Art Project gave an opportunity to muralists eager for a chance to work in the style of Rivera, Orozco, and Siqueiros. The Federal Art Project fostered the careers of painters like Stuart Davis, Raphael Soyer, Yasuo Kuniyoshi, and Jackson Pollock. Out of the same project came a network of community art centers and the notable *Index of American Design*. A generation later the sculptor Louise

Nevelson summed up what it meant:

> When I came back from Germany where I studied with
> Hans Hoffman . . . I got on the WPA. Now that gave me a
> certain kind of freedom and I think that our great artists like
> Rothko, de Kooning, Franz Kline, all these people that have
> promise today and are creative, had that moment of peace . . .
> to continue with their work. So, I feel that that was a great
> benefit, a great contribution to our creative people and very
> important in the history of art. And not only in the visual arts
> but in the theater, and the folk arts, there wasn't a thing that
> they didn't touch on. . . . At that period, people in our coun-
> try didn't have jobs and the head of government was able so
> intelligently to use mankind and manpower. I think it's a
> high-light of our American history.

The Federal Writers' Project provided support for scores
of talented novelists and poets, editors and literary critics,
men like Ralph Ellison and Nelson Algren, John Cheever
and Saul Bellow. These writers turned out an exceptional set
of state guides . . . and special volumes like *These Are Our
Lives*, a graphic portfolio of life histories in North Carolina.
. . . Project workers transcribed chain-gang blues songs, recovered folklore that would otherwise have been lost, and
collected the narratives of elderly former slaves, an invalu-
able archive later published in *Lay My Burden Down*. When
the magazine *Story* conducted a contest for the best contribution by a Project employee, the prize was won by an un-
published 29-year-old black who had been working on the
essay on the Negro for the Illinois guide. With the prize
money for his stories, subsequently published as *Uncle Tom's
Children*, Richard Wright gained the time to complete his
remarkable first novel, *Native Son*.

Some thought it an ill omen that the Federal Theatre Project's first production was Shakespeare's *Comedy of Errors*, but
that agency not only gave employment to actors and stage
technicians but offered many communities their first glimpse
of live drama. The "boy wonder" Orson Welles directed and
acted in the Federal Theatre, which also discovered such un-
knowns as Joseph Cotten. Its Dance Group revealed the vir-

tuosity of Katherine Dunham, Doris Humphrey, and Charles Weidman. The Federal Theatre sponsored the first U.S. presentation of T.S. Eliot's *Murder in the Cathedral*, and its Detroit unit staged the original professional production of [*Death of a Salesman* author] Arthur Miller's first play.

If the creation of America's first state theatre was an unusual departure, the New Deal's ventures in documentary films seemed no less surprising. With Resettlement Administration funds, Pare Lorentz produced *The Plow That Broke the Plains* in 1936 and the classic *The River* in 1937. He engaged cameramen like Paul Strand, who had won acclaim for his movie on a fisherman's strike in Mexico; invited the young composer Virgil Thomson, who had just scored Gertrude Stein's *Four Saints in Three Acts*, to compose the background music; and employed Thomas Chalmers, who had sung at the Metropolitan Opera in the era of Caruso, to read the narration. Lorentz's films were eye-openers. American government documentaries before the New Deal had been limited to short subjects on topics like the love life of the honeybee. *The River*, which won first prize in Venice at the International Exposition of Cinematographic Art in 1938, proved that there was an audience in the United States for well-wrought documentaries. By 1940 it had drawn more than 10 million people, while *The Plow That Broke the Plains*, said one critic, made "the rape of millions of acres . . . more moving than the downfall of a Hollywood blonde."

Strides in Forestry and Agriculture

Lorentz's films suggest the concern of the New Deal for the American land. Roosevelt, it has been said, had a "proprietary interest in the nation's estate," and this helps account for the fact that the 1930s accomplished for soil conservation and river valley development what the era of Theodore Roosevelt had done for the forests. The Tennessee Valley Authority, which drew admirers from all over the world, put the national government in the business of generating electric power, controlled floods, terraced hillsides, and gave new hope to the people of the valley. In the Pacific Northwest the PWA constructed mammoth dams, Grand Coulee and Bonneville. Roosevelt's "tree army," the Civilian Conservation Corps, planted millions of trees, cleared forest trails, laid out picnic sites and campgrounds, and aided the Forest Service in the vast undertaking of establishing a shelterbelt—a windbreak of trees and shrubs: green ash and Chinese elm, apricot and blackberry, buffalo berry and Osage orange from the Canadian border to the Texas panhandle. Government agencies came to the aid of drought-stricken farmers in the Dust Bowl, and the Soil Conservation Service, another New Deal creation, instructed growers in methods of cultivation to save the land. As Alistair Cooke later said, the favorite of the New Dealers was the farmer with the will to "take up contour plowing late in life."

These services to farmers represented only a small part of the government's program, for in the New Deal years, the business of agriculture was revolutionized. Roosevelt came to power at a time of mounting desperation for American farmers. Each month in 1932 another 20,000 farmers had lost their land because of inability to meet their debts in a period of collapsing prices. On a single day in May 1932, one-fourth of the state of Mississippi went under the sheriff's hammer. The Farm Credit Administration of 1933 came to the aid of the beleaguered farmer, and within eighteen months, it had refinanced one-fifth of all farm mortgages in the United States. In the Roosevelt years, too, the Rural Electrification Administration literally brought rural America out of darkness. At the beginning of the Roosevelt era, only one farm in nine had electricity; at the end, only one in nine did not have it. But more important than any of these developments was the progression of enactments starting with the first AAA (the Agricultural Adjustment Act) of 1933, which began the process of granting large-scale subsidies to growers. As William Faulkner later said, "Our economy is not agricultural any longer. Our economy is the federal government. We no longer farm in Mississippi cotton fields. We farm now in Washington corridors and Congressional committee rooms."

At the same time that its realm was being expanded under the New Deal, the national government changed the composition of its personnel and of its beneficiaries. Before 1933, the government had paid heed primarily to a single group—white Anglo-Saxon Protestant males. The Roosevelt Administration, however, recruited from a more ethnically diverse group . . . [including] Catholics and Jews among the President's advisers. . . . The Federal Writers' Project turned out books on Italians and Albanians, and the Federal Theatre staged productions in Yiddish and wrote a history of the Chinese stage in Los Angeles. In the 1930s women played a more prominent role in government than they ever had before, as the result of such appointments as that of Frances Perkins as the first female cabinet member, while the influence of Eleanor Roosevelt was pervasive.

Before Eleanor Roosevelt, First Ladies had been content to preside over the social functions of the White House. But by 1940 Mrs. Roosevelt had travelled more than 250,000 miles, written 1 million words, and became the leading advocate within the administration for the underprivileged, especially blacks and unemployed youth. No one knew where she would turn up next. In the most famous cartoon of the decade, a begrimed coal miner in the bowels of the earth cries out in astonishment to a fellow miner, "For gosh sakes, here comes Mrs. Roosevelt." Admiral Byrd, it was said, always set up two places for dinner at the South Pole "in case Eleanor should drop in." She was renowned for her informality. When the King and Queen of England visited America, she served them hot dogs and beer, and when during World War II, she travelled to Australia and New Zealand, she greeted her Maori guide by rubbing noses. No one captured the goals of the New Deal better than Eleanor Roosevelt. "As I have said all along," she remarked, "you have got to have the kind of country in which people's daily chance convinces them that democracy is a good thing."

Although in some respects the New Deal's performance with regard to blacks added to the sorry record of racial discrimination in America, important gains were also registered in the 1930s. Blacks, who had often been excluded from relief in the past, now received a share of WPA jobs considerably greater than their proportion of the population. Blacks moved into federal housing projects; federal funds went to schools and hospitals in black neighborhoods; and New Deal agencies like the Farm Security Administration (FSA) enabled 50,000 Negro tenant farmers and sharecroppers to become proprietors. "Indeed," one historian has written, "there is a high correlation between the location of extensive FSA operations in the 1930s and the rapidity of political modernization in black communities in the South in the 1960s." Roosevelt appointed a number of blacks, including William Hastie, Mary McLeod Bethune, and Robert Weaver, to high posts in the government. Negroes in the South who were disfranchised in white primaries voted in AAA crop referenda and in National Labor Relations Board plant elections, and a step was taken toward restoring their constitutional rights when Attorney General Frank Murphy set up a Civil Liberties Unit in the Department of Justice. The reign of Jim Crow in Washington offices, which had begun under Roosevelt's Democratic predecessor, Woodrow Wilson, was terminated by Secretary of the Interior Harold Ickes who desegregated cafeterias in his department. Ickes also had a role in the most dramatic episode of the times, for when the Daughters of the American Revolution (DAR) denied the use of their concert hall to the black contralto Marian Anderson, he made it possible for her to sing before thousands from the steps of Lincoln Memorial; and Mrs. Roosevelt joined in the rebuke to the DAR. Anderson's concert on Easter Sunday 1939 was heard by thousands at the Memorial, and three networks carried her voice to millions more. Blacks delivered their own verdict on the New Deal at the polling places. Committed to the party of Lincoln as late as 1932, when they voted overwhelmingly for Hoover, they shifted in large numbers to the party of FDR during Roosevelt's first term. This was a change of allegiance that many whites were also making in those years.

The Durable Legacy of the New Deal

The Great Depression and the New Deal brought about a significant political realignment of the sort that occurs only rarely in America. The Depression wrenched many lifelong

Republican voters from their moorings. In 1928, one couple christened their newborn son "Herbert Hoover Jones." Four years later they petitioned the court, "desiring to relieve the young man from the chagrin and mortification which he is suffering and will suffer," and asked that his name be changed to Franklin D. Roosevelt Jones. In 1932 FDR became the first Democrat to enter the White House with as much as 50 percent of the popular vote in eighty years—since Franklin K. Pierce in 1852. Roosevelt took advantage of this opportunity to mold "the FDR coalition," an alliance centered in the low-income districts of the great cities and, as recently as the 1980 election, the contours of the New Deal coalition could still be discerned. Indeed, over the past half-century, the once overpowering Republicans have won control of Congress only twice, for a total of four years. No less important was the shift in the character of the Democratic party from the conservative organization of John W. Davis and John J. Raskob to the country's main political instrumentality for reform. "One political result of the Roosevelt years," Robert Burke has observed, "was a basic change in the nature of the typical Congressional liberal." He was no longer a maverick, who made a fetish of orneriness, no longer one of the men Senator Moses called "the sons of the wild jackass," but "a party Democrat, labor-oriented, urban, and internationalist-minded."

Furthermore, the New Deal drastically altered the agenda of American politics. When Arthur Krock of the *New York Times* listed the main programmatic questions before the 1932 Democratic convention, he wrote: "What would be said about the repeal of prohibition that had split the Republicans? What would be said about tariffs?" By 1936, these concerns seemed altogether old-fashioned, as campaigners discussed the Tennessee Valley Authority and industrial relations, slum clearance and aid to the jobless. That year, a Little Rock newspaper commented: "Such matters as tax and tariff laws have given way to universally human things, the living problems and opportunities of the average man and the average family.". . .

What then did the New Deal do? It gave far greater amplitude to the national state, expanded the authority of the presidency, recruited university-trained administrators, won control of the money supply, established central banking, imposed regulation on Wall Street, rescued the debt-ridden farmer and homeowner, built model communities, financed the Federal Housing Administration, made federal housing a permanent feature, fostered unionization of the factories, reduced child labor, ended the tyranny of company towns, wiped out many sweatshops, mandated minimal working standards, enabled tenants to buy their own farms, built camps for migrants, introduced the welfare state with old-age pensions, unemployment insurance, and aid for dependent children, provided jobs for millions of unemployed, created a special program for the jobless young and for students, covered the American landscape with new edifices, subsidized painters and novelists, composers and ballet dancers, founded America's first state theater, created documentary films, gave birth to the impressive Tennessee Valley Authority, generated electrical power, sent the Civilian Conservation Corps boys into the forests, initiated the Soil Conservation Service, transformed the economy of agriculture, lighted up rural America, gave women greater recognition, made a start toward breaking the pattern of racial discrimination and segregation, put together a liberal party coalition, changed the agenda of American politics, and brought about a Constitutional Revolution.

But even this summary does not account for the full range of its activities. The New Deal offered the American Indian new opportunities for self-government and established the Indian Arts and Crafts Board, sponsored vaudeville troupes and circuses, . . . was responsible for the founding of the Buffalo Philharmonic, the Oklahoma Symphony, and the Utah State Symphony, served hot lunches to school children and set up hundreds of nursery schools, sent bookmobiles into isolated communities, and where there were no roads, had books carried in by packhorses. And only a truly merciful and farsighted government would have taken such special pains to find jobs for unemployed historians.

The New Deal accomplished all of this at a critical time,

when many were insisting that fascism was the wave of the future and denying that democracy could be effective. For those throughout the world who heard such jeremiads [complaints] with foreboding, the American experience was enormously inspiriting. . . .

By restoring to the debate over the significance of the New Deal acknowledgment of its achievements, we may hope to produce a more judicious estimate of where it succeeded and where it failed. For it unquestionably did fail in a number of respects. There were experiments of the 1930s which miscarried, opportunities that were fumbled, groups who were neglected, and power that was arrogantly used. Over the whole performance lies the dark cloud of the persistence of hard times. The shortcomings of the New Deal are formidable, and they must be recognized. But I am not persuaded that the New Deal experience was negligible. Indeed, it is hard to think of another period in the whole history of the republic that was so fruitful or of a crisis that was met with as much imagination.

Appendix

Excerpts from Original Documents Pertaining to the Great Depression

Document 1: Herbert Hoover Endorses Self-Reliance

In October 1928, near the close of the presidential election campaign, Republican candidate Herbert Hoover delivered his now famous "rugged individualism" speech, excerpted here, in which he touted the "American system" of self-reliance and decried the evils of an intrusive, overcontrolling government.

During 150 years we have builded up a form of self-government and a social system which is peculiarly our own. It differs essentially from all others in the world. It is the American system. It is just as definite and positive a political and social system as has ever been developed on earth. It is founded upon a particular conception of self-government in which decentralized local responsibility is the very base. Further than this, it is founded upon the conception that only through ordered liberty, freedom and equal opportunity to the individual will his initiative and enterprise spur on the march of progress. And in our insistence upon equality of opportunity has our system advanced beyond all the world.

During the war we necessarily turned to the Government to solve every difficult economic problem. The Government having absorbed every energy of our people for war, there was no other solution. For the preservation of the State the Federal Government became a centralized despotism which undertook unprecedented responsibilities, assumed autocratic powers, and took over the business of citizens. To a large degree we regimented our whole people temporarily into a socialistic state. However justified in time of war if continued in peace time it would destroy not only our American system but with it our progress and freedom as well.

When the war closed, the most vital of all issues both in our own country and throughout the world was whether Governments should continue their wartime ownership and operation of many instrumentalities of production and distribution. We were challenged with a peace-time choice between the American system of rugged individualism and a European philosophy of diametrically opposed doctrines—doctrines of paternalism and state socialism. The acceptance of these ideas would have meant the destruction of self-government through centralization of government. It would have meant the undermining of the individual initiative and enterprise through which our people have grown to unparalleled greatness.

The Republican Party from the beginning resolutely turned its face away from these ideas and these war practices. . . . When the Republican Party came into full power it went at once resolutely back to our fundamental conception of the State and the rights and responsibilities of the individual. . . .

There has been revived in this campaign, however, a series of proposals which, if adopted, would be a long step toward the abandonment of our American system and a surrender to the destructive operation of governmental conduct of commercial business. . . .

There is, therefore, submitted to the American people a question of fundamental principle. That is: shall we depart from the principles of our American political and economic system, upon which we have advanced beyond all the rest of the world, in order to adopt methods based on principles destructive of its very foundations? And I wish to emphasize the seriousness of these proposals. I wish to make my position clear; for this goes to the very roots of American life and progress.

I should like to state to you the effect that this projection of government in business would have upon our system of self-government and our economic system. That effect would reach to the daily life of every man and woman. It would impair the very basis of liberty and freedom not only for those left outside the fold of expanded bureaucracy but for those embraced within it.

Let us first see the effect upon self-government. When the Federal Government undertakes to go into commercial business it must at once set up the organization and administration of that business, and it immediately finds itself in a labyrinth, every alley of which leads to the destruction of self-government.

Commercial business requires a concentration of responsibility. Self-government requires decentralization and many checks and balances to safeguard liberty. Our Government to succeed in business would need become in effect a despotism. There at once begins the destruction of self-government. . . .

It is a false liberalism that interprets itself into the Government operation of commercial business. Every step of bureaucratizing of the business of our country poisons the very roots of liberalism—that is, political equality, free speech, free assembly, free press, and equality of opportunity. It is the road not to more liberty, but to less liberty. Liberalism should be found not striving to spread bureaucracy but striving to set bounds to it. True liberalism seeks all legitimate freedom, first in the confident belief that without such freedom the pursuit of all other blessings and benefits is vain. That belief is the foundation of all American progress, political as well as economic. . . .

Our people have the right to know whether we can continue to solve our great problems without abandonment of our American system. I know we can. . . .

And what have been the results of our American system? Our country has become the land of opportunity to those born without inheritance, not merely because of the wealth of its resources and industry, but because of this freedom of initiative and enterprise. . . .

By adherence to the principles of decentralized self-government, ordered liberty, equal opportunity and freedom to the individual, our American experiment in human welfare has yielded a degree of well-being unparalleled in all the world. It has come nearer to the abolition of poverty, to the abolition of fear of want, than humanity has ever reached before. Progress of the past seven years is the proof of it. This alone furnishes the answer to our opponents who ask us to introduce destructive elements into the system by which this has been accomplished. . . .

I have endeavored to present to you that the greatness of America has grown out of a political and social system and a method of control of economic forces distinctly its own—our American system—which has carried this great experiment in human welfare further than ever before in all history. We are nearer today to the ideal of the abolition of poverty and fear from the lives of men and women than ever before in any land. And I again repeat that the departure from our American system by injecting principles destructive to it which our opponents propose will jeopardize the very liberty and freedom of our people, will destroy equality of opportunity, not alone to ourselves but to our children.

Quoted in Richard Hofstadter, ed., *Great Issues in American History: A Documentary Record*. vol. 2: *1864–1957*. New York: Vintage Books, 1960, pp. 338–43.

Document 2: The Failure of Relief Efforts

In May 1932, with unemployment, hunger, and other ravages of the depression steadily worsening, Joseph L. Heffernan, mayor of Youngstown, Ohio, penned this tract, which is both a lament on the failure of relief efforts and a warning about the potential long-term harm posed to American self-esteem by the need to resort to taking charity.

Often, as I have watched the line of job seekers at the City Hall, I have had occasion to marvel at the mysterious power that certain words and phrases exercise upon the human mind. A wise man once observed that words rule mankind, and so it is in America today. Prominent politicians and business men have repeatedly stated that, come what may, America must not have the dole. To be sure, we should all be much happier if we could get along without a dole, but the simple truth is that we have it already. Every city in the land has had a dole from the moment it began unemployment relief. The men who apply for help know that it is a dole. The officials who issue work orders can be in no doubt about it, for the work done in no way justifies the money spent, except on the basis of a dole.

Why, then, so much concern about the word? Perhaps because, if we were honest enough to recognize unemployment relief for the dole it really is, we should also have to be honest enough to admit that the depression is a catastrophe of historic proportions, and courageous enough to deal with it accordingly. One alternative to the dole would be to let all the unfortunates starve to death, but so far no one has advanced this proposal, although some have come pretty close to it in saying that the way out of the depression is to let nature take its course.

Those who have not been willing to go so far as that have maintained, however, that each community must look after its own unemployed, and that under no circumstances must the Federal Government assume any responsibility for them. For two years local communities have carried the burden unassisted, and many of them, like Youngstown, have prostrated themselves in doing it. We of the cities have done our best, laboring against conditions which were beyond our control. But, even if we are given full credit for trying, we must now admit that we have failed miserably. Whether this was caused by a lack of simple charity in the hearts of our people or by our incapacity to manage our financial problems is beside the point. The fact of our failure is patent. We of the cities have not advanced a single new idea on unemployment or its relief. We have not dared to consider the fundamental questions raised by our social and economic collapse. We are still as stupidly devoted as ever to the philosophy of *laissez faire*, and we face the future bewildered and purposeless. Our one great achievement in response to this national catastrophe has been to open soup kitchens and flop-houses.

And nobody has taken the trouble to weigh the consequences of our well-meant but ineffective charity upon the moral fibre of the American people. Seventy years ago we fought a civil war to free black slaves; to-day we remain indifferent while millions of our fellow citizens are reduced to the status of paupers. There is a world of difference between mere poverty and pauperism. The honest poor will struggle for years to keep themselves above the pauper class. With quiet desperation they will bear hunger and mental anguish until every resource is exhausted. Then comes the ultimate struggle when, with heartache and an overwhelming sense of disgrace, they have to make the shamefaced journey to the door of public charity. This is the last straw. Their self-respect is destroyed; they undergo an insidious metamorphosis, and sink down to spiritless despondency.

This descent from respectability, frequent enough in the best of times, has been hastened immeasurably by two years of business paralysis, and the people who have been affected in this manner must be numbered in millions. This is what we have accomplished with our bread lines and soup kitchens. I know, because I have seen thousands of these defeated, discouraged, hopeless men and women, cringing and fawning as they come to ask for public aid. It is a spectacle of national degeneration. That is the fundamental tragedy for America. If every mill and factory in the land should begin to hum with prosperity to-morrow morning, the destructive effect of our haphazard relief measures would not work itself out of the nation's blood until the sons of our sons have expiated the sins of our neglect.

Joseph L. Heffernan, "The Hungry City: A Mayor's Experience with Unemployment," *Atlantic Monthly*, May 1932.

Document 3: Roosevelt Promises Americans a New Deal

In accepting the Democratic Party's nomination for the presidency on July 2, 1932, Franklin D. Roosevelt, then governor of New York State, promised the American people that the policies of the past were about to end and that a better future was about to begin. In the conclusion of the speech, he coined the term "New Deal," which would ever after be synonymous with his presidency.

At last our eyes are open. At last the American people are ready to acknowledge that Republican leadership was wrong and that the Democracy is right.

My program, of which I can only touch on these points, is based upon this simple moral principle: the welfare and the soundness of a Nation depend first upon what the great mass of the people wish and need; and second, whether or not they are getting it.

What do the people of America want more than anything else? To my mind, they want two things: work, with all the moral and spiritual values that go with it; and with work, a reasonable measure of security—security for themselves and for their wives and children. Work and security—these are more than words. They are more than facts. They are the spiritual values, the true goal toward which our efforts of reconstruction should lead. These are the values that this program is intended to gain; these are the values we have failed to achieve by the leadership we now have.

Our Republican leaders tell us economic laws—sacred, inviolable, unchangeable—cause panics which no one could prevent. But while they prate of economic laws, men and women are starving. We must lay hold of the fact that economic laws are not made by nature. They are made by human beings. . . .

I say that while primary responsibility for relief rests with localities now, as ever, yet the Federal Government has always had and still has a continuing responsibility for the broader public welfare. It will soon fulfill that responsibility. . . .

Never before in modern history have the essential differences between the two major American parties stood out in such striking contrast as they do today. Republican leaders not only have failed in material things, they have failed in national vision, because in disaster they have held out no hope, they have pointed out no path for the people below to climb back to places of security and of safety in our American life.

Throughout the Nation, men and women, forgotten in the political philosophy of the Government of the last years look to us here for guidance and for more equitable opportunity to share in the distribution of national wealth.

On the farms, in the large metropolitan areas, in the smaller cities and in the villages, millions of our citizens cherish the hope that their old standards of living and of thought have not gone forever. Those millions cannot and shall not hope in vain.

I pledge you, I pledge myself, to a new deal for the American people. Let us all here assembled constitute ourselves prophets of a new order of competence and of courage. This is more than a political campaign; it is a call to arms. Give me your help, not to win votes alone, but to win in this crusade to restore America to its own people.

Samuel I. Rosenman, ed., *The Public Papers and Addresses of Franklin D. Roosevelt*. New York: Russell and Russell, 1969, vol. 1, pp. 657–59.

Document 4: Hoover and Roosevelt on Inauguration Day

James Roosevelt, F.D.R.'s son, here reminisces about outgoing president Herbert Hoover's "stonefaced" demeanor while riding to the inauguration ceremonies with president-elect Franklin Roosevelt.

To return now to the early days of the New Deal, my real introduction to the operation was on inauguration day, fifty years ago on the 4th of March. Two days earlier, we had paid a courtesy call on President Hoover, as the incoming President is called upon to do. It was rather a tense moment, because my father had refused to participate in any of the final moves that President Hoover was proposing, and President Hoover didn't like this. He thought it was unpatriotic, and he felt it was unfair to him, because he wanted to leave his stamp on the efforts to get out of the Depression.

My father felt that this was not a wise thing to do, that he ought to come in with a clean slate, not linked in any way to the past, and he steadfastly refused to join hands with President Hoover's recommendations. So when we went over to pay this call about four o'clock in the afternoon, my father knew there were problems ahead. We were seated in the green room on the ground floor, and after about half an hour, which seemed to me a rather long time to keep an incoming President waiting, President and Mrs. Hoover came downstairs and came into the room, and there they were joined by the Secretary of the Treasury, Mr. Mills.

My father whispered to me, "Uh-oh. They're going to have one more try." And sure enough they had one more try, and again the proposal was turned down. So after about ten minutes, Father saw that the President was getting a little nervous, and so he said, "Mr. President, I guess it's time we should take our leave. I hope you'll understand that my heavy braces make it impossible for me to move very quickly, and so if you don't mind, I'll just stay seated until you and Mrs. Hoover have retired, and then I'll take myself and my family down below."

President Hoover drew himself up and in rather a clearcut voice said, "Mr. Roosevelt, when you become President you'll find out that nobody leaves the room before the President of the United States." Two days later, when we were driving to the Capitol for the inauguration, there were quite a few people on the sidewalk and along the route, and I noticed that my father was taking off his hat and bowing and answering the people who were greeting him on the side. Mr. Hoover was sitting there absolutely stonefaced and not saying a word to anybody. As we went by the new Archives Building, which was about one-third completed, I suddenly heard my father say, "Mr. President, isn't that beautiful steel in that new building?" And Mr. Hoover went, "Huh." And that was the total conversation from the White House to the Capitol that day.

Quoted in Wilbur J. Cohen, *The New Deal Fifty Years After: A Historical Assessment.* Austin, TX: Lyndon Baines Johnson Library, 1984, pp. 46–47.

Document 5: Roosevelt Declares War on the Depression

Following are excerpts from Franklin D. Roosevelt's first inaugural address, delivered on March 4, 1933, in which he galvanized the nation with a stirring call to "wage a war" against the economic and social crisis the nation then faced.

This is a day of national consecration, and I am certain that my fellow-Americans expect that on my induction into the Presidency I will address them with a candor and a decision which the present situation of our nation impels.

This is pre-eminently the time to speak the truth, the whole truth, frankly and boldly. Nor need we shrink from honestly facing conditions in our country today. This great nation will endure as it has endured, will revive and will prosper.

So first of all let me assert my firm belief that the only thing we have to fear is fear itself—nameless, unreasoning, unjustified terror which paralyzes needed efforts to convert retreat into advance.

In every dark hour of our national life a leadership of frankness and vigor has met with that understanding and support of the people themselves which is essential to victory. I am convinced that you will again give that support to leadership in these critical days. . . .

Our greatest primary task is to put people to work. This is no unsolvable problem if we face it wisely and courageously.

It can be accomplished in part by direct recruiting by the government itself, treating the task as we would treat the emergency of a war, but at the same time, through this employment, accomplishing greatly needed projects to stimulate and reorganize the use of our natural resources.

Hand in hand with this, we must frankly recognize the overbalance of population in our industrial centers and, by engaging on a national scale in a redistribution, endeavor to provide a better use of the land for those best fitted for the land. . . .

If I read the temper of our people correctly, we now realize as we have never realized before, our interdependence on each other; that we cannot merely take, but we must give as well; that if we are to go forward we must move as a trained and loyal army willing to sacrifice for the good of a common discipline, because, without such discipline, no progress is made, no leadership becomes effective.

We are, I know, ready and willing to submit our lives and property to such discipline because it makes possible a leadership which aims at a larger good.

This I propose to offer, pledging that the larger purposes will bind upon us all as a sacred obligation with a unity of duty hitherto evoked only in time of armed strife.

With this pledge taken, I assume unhesitatingly the leadership of this great army of our people, dedicated to a disciplined attack upon our common problems. . . .

It is to be hoped that the normal balance of executive and legislative authority may be wholly adequate to meet the unprecedented task before us. But it may be that an unprecedented demand and need for undelayed action may call for temporary departure from that normal balance of public procedure.

I am prepared under my constitutional duty to recommend the measures that a stricken nation in the midst of a stricken world may require.

These measures, or such other measures as the Congress may build out of its experience and wisdom, I shall seek, within my constitutional authority, to bring to speedy adoption. . . .

I shall ask the Congress for the one remaining instrument to meet the crisis—broad executive power to wage a war against the emergency as great as the power that would be given to me if we were in fact invaded by a foreign foe.

For the trust reposed in me I will return the courage and the devotion that befit the time. I can do no less.

We face the arduous days that lie before us in the warm courage of national unity; with the clear consciousness of seeking old and precious moral values; with the clean satisfaction that comes from the stern performance of duty by old and young alike. . . .

In this dedication of a nation we humbly ask the blessing of God. May He protect each and every one of us! May He guide me in the days to come!

Quoted in Richard Hofstadter, ed., *Great Issues in American History: A Documentary Record*. vol. 2: *1864–1957*. New York: Vintage Books, 1960, pp. 352–57.

Document 6: Acts of Violence Underscore the People's Desperation

These excerpts from an April 27, 1933, AP news release, less than two months after Roosevelt took office as president, graphically illustrate the serious national morale problem he was faced with alleviating.

A crowd of more than 100 farmers late today dragged District Judge Charles C. Bradley from his courtroom, slapped him, carried him blindfolded in a truck to a crossroads a mile from here, put a rope around his neck, choked him until he was only partly conscious, smeared grease on his face and stole his trousers.

The abduction occurred after the judge had refused to swear he would sign no more farm mortgage foreclosures.

The story of the abduction was related by a news correspondent who accompanied the farmers and who remained with Judge Bradley throughout the entire affair.

Shortly after 4 p.m., the farmers entered the judge's courtroom to discuss with him hearings which are to determine the constitutionality of two new laws relating to mortgage foreclosures.

The judge requested them to take off their hats and to stop smoking.

"This is my court," he said.

The farmers rose in reply to his demands, dragged him off the bench, slapped him and shook him and carried him bodily out of the court room, through the lobby of the courthouse and on to the lawn.

There they demanded that he "swear" not to sign any more foreclosure actions. Judge Bradley, about 60 years old, defied the crowd. He was roughly handled.

When he persisted in refusing to give the oath, the farmers, most of whom then were masked, loaded the blindfolded judge into a truck, climbed in behind him and carried him away. At a crossroads about one mile southeast of Le Mars, they put a rope around his neck, the witness related, and repeated their demands. The judge still refused and one of the farmers tugged on the rope.

Judge Bradley fell, only partly conscious, but still refusing to comply with the demands. The farmers dragged the judge to his feet, carried him to the side of the road and threw the loose end of the rope over a sign.

"Make him get down on his knees and pray," one of the farmers shouted.

The judge was pushed to his knees and declared:

"I will do the fair thing to all men to the best of my knowledge."

One of the farmers removed a hub cap from a nearby truck, partly filled with oil, and placed it on the judge's head. The oil and grease ran down his face as farmers threw dirt, which stuck to the oil.

The farmers removed the judge's trousers and filled them with dirt, then drove off, leaving the begrimed jurist standing in the middle of the road. Several offered him a ride, which he refused. His neck was chafed and his lips were bloody, in addition to the dirt and grease on his face and hair.

He was taken back to town in a car by Wilbur DePress, son of the Rev. J.J. DePress. Arriving at the courthouse, he asked to be left alone.

"I'd rather not say," he replied in answer to queries as to whether he would seek prosecution for his abductors. . . .

Earlier in the day, farmers, reported to be the same persons who participated in the abduction, were held off by 22 deputies at Primghar, Iowa, while Sheriff Ed Leemkull directed the sale of the John Shaffer farm.

The farmers stormed the O'Brien County courthouse, but the efforts of the deputies held them to the two lower floors while the sale was completed. The farm, 160 acres near Calumet, Iowa, brought $6,500.

O.R. Montzhelmer, attorney for the mortgage holders, was seized as he left the courthouse and forced to kiss the American flag and to promise not to bring further foreclosure actions.

After returning from Primghar, the delegation of Plymouth County farmers seized Clarence Becker, mortgage holder in another foreclosure action, carried him to the ballpark grounds and threatened him with a rope. Sheriff Rippey persuaded them to disperse, and they proceeded to Judge Bradley's chambers.

Quoted in Associated Press Writers, *The Great Depression, 1929–1939*. Danbury, CT: Grolier, 1995, pp. 35–36.

Document 7: The President Restores Confidence in the Banks

This is an excerpt from Roosevelt's first fireside chat, delivered over the radio on March 12, 1933 (just eight days after he had assumed the presidency), in which he explained to the American people why he had declared a "bank holiday" and urged them to remain confident in the existing banking system. His effort was largely successful.

This bank holiday, while resulting in many cases in great inconvenience, is affording us the opportunity to supply the currency necessary to meet the situation. No sound bank is a dollar worse off than it was when it closed its doors last Monday. Neither is any bank which may turn out not to be in a position for immediate opening. The new law allows the twelve Federal Reserve Banks to issue additional currency on good assets and thus the banks which reopen will be able to meet every legitimate call. The new currency is being sent out by the Bureau of Engraving and Printing in large volume to every part of the country. It is sound currency because it is backed by actual, good assets.

A question you will ask is this: why are all the banks not to be reopened at the same time? The answer is simple. Your Government does not intend that the history of the past few years shall be repeated. We do not want and will not have another epidemic of bank failures.

As a result, we start tomorrow, Monday, with the opening of banks in the twelve Federal Reserve Bank cities—those banks which on first examination by the Treasury have already been found to be all right. This will be followed on Tuesday by the resumption of all their functions by banks already found to be sound in cities where there are recognized clearing houses. That means about 250 cities of the United States.

On Wednesday and succeeding days banks in smaller places all through the country will resume business, subject, of course, to the Government's physical ability to complete its survey. It is necessary that the reopening of banks be extended over a period in order to permit the banks to make applications for necessary loans, to obtain currency needed to meet their requirements and to enable the Government to make common sense checkups.

Let me make it clear to you that if your bank does not open the first day you are by no means justified in believing that it will not open. A bank that opens on one of the subsequent days is in exactly the same status as the bank that opens tomorrow. . . .

It is possible that when the banks resume a very few people who have not recovered from their fear may again begin withdrawals. Let me make it clear that the banks will take care of all needs—and it is my belief that hoarding during the past week has become an exceedingly unfashionable pastime. It needs no prophet to tell you that when the people find that they can get their money—that they can get it when they want it for all legitimate purposes—the phantom of fear will soon be laid. People will again be glad to have their money where it will be safely taken care of and where they can use it conveniently at any time. I can assure you that it is safer to keep your money in a reopened bank than under the mattress.

The success of our whole great national program depends, of course, upon the cooperation of the public—on its intelligent support and use of a reliable system. . . .

We had a bad banking situation. Some of our bankers had

shown themselves either incompetent or dishonest in their handling of the people's funds. They had used the money entrusted to them in speculations and unwise loans. This was, of course, not true in the vast majority of our banks, but it was true in enough of them to shock the people for a time into a sense of insecurity and to put them into a frame of mind where they did not differentiate, but seemed to assume that the acts of a comparative few had tainted them all. It was the Government's job to straighten out this situation and do it as quickly as possible. And the job is being performed. . . .

It has been wonderful to me to catch the note of confidence from all over the country. I can never be sufficiently grateful to the people for the loyal support they have given me in their acceptance of the judgment that has dictated our course, even though all our processes may not have seemed clear to them.

After all, there is an element in the readjustment of our financial system more important than currency, more important than gold, and that is the confidence of the people. Confidence and courage are the essentials of success in carrying out our plan. You people must have faith; you must not be stampeded by rumors or guesses. Let us unite in banishing fear. We have provided the machinery to restore our financial system; it is up to you to support and make it work.

It is your problem no less than it is mine. Together we cannot fail.

Quoted in Daniel Aaron and Robert Bendiner, eds., *The Strenuous Decade: A Social and Intellectual Record of the 1930s.* Garden City, NY: Doubleday, 1970, pp. 92–94.

Document 8: Congress Passes the TVA

This May 17, 1933, AP news item records some of the details of Congress's approval of one of the first New Deal programs, the Tennessee Valley Authority (TVA), the massive hydroelectric project that would, in succeeding years, build numerous dams and bring inexpensive electricity to large tracts of rural America.

Congress put its final approval on the administration's vast Muscle Shoals-Tennessee basin development bill today, and only President Roosevelt's signature remained to be affixed before the new law on the expanded wartime project takes effect.

House adoption, 259 to 112, of the Senate-approved conference report embodying the principal provisions of the Norris bill, ended congressional action.

It was the first such bill to be approved by Congress that also was favored by the White House.

It fulfills a Democratic Party platform pledge, carries out one of President Roosevelt's urgent requests for emergency legislation and puts a government corporation into the power production business.

Delay in sending the engrossed bill to the White House was caused by early adjournment of the House, in respect to the death of Rep. Charles Brand of Georgia, which prevented Speaker William Rainey and Vice President Garner from affixing their signatures.

Chairman John J. McSwain (D-S.C.) of the House Military Committee said the bill would be taken to the White House for Mr. Roosevelt's signature tomorrow.

Eleven Republicans and three Farmer-Laborites joined 245 Democrats in support, while 28 Democrats voted with 84 Republicans against the bill.

The measure provides for creation of a board of three, to be appointed by the president to direct the Tennessee Valley Authority. This corporation will handle the vast project, including production of power and fertilizer at Muscle Shoals on the Tennessee River, construction of a power dam on Cove Creek in Tennessee and building and purchase of transmission lines.

Quoted in Associated Press Writers, *The Great Depression, 1929–1939.* Danbury, CT: Grolier, 1995, p. 97.

Document 9: The Problem of Huge Farm Surpluses

Here, from his acclaimed biography of Franklin Roosevelt, scholar Kenneth S. Davis lists the vast acreages of various crops planted by American farmers in the spring of 1933. The size of these tracts was counterproductive at the time because most farmers were able to sell only a fraction of their harvests. The Agricultural Adjustment Act (AAA) was designed to help alleviate this problem by significantly reducing the number of acres in production and thereby, hopefully, increasing the worth of the resulting smaller harvests.

When the agricultural adjustment bill was introduced in the Seventy-third Congress in mid-March, Roosevelt had pressed Congress for its speedy enactment so that it could have effect before spring planting of crops had been completed. Congress had not been able to move at anything like that speed upon a measure so complicated and controversial. By May 12, when the bill was at last signed into law, corn was growing on nearly 106,000,000 acres, wheat (most of it winter wheat, planted in 1932) on nearly

50,000,000 acres, and cotton on nearly 40,000,000 acres. These were far larger acreages than were needed, if per acre production was anywhere near normal and if need was defined as effective market demand. The last year, from nearly 58,000,000 acres, wheat farmers had harvested 756,000,000 bushels, and of this huge crop almost half (360,000,000 bushels) remained unconsumed—a carryover three and a half times that of former years. Last year from nearly 36,000,000 acres, cotton farmers had harvested a little more than 13,000,000 bales, and 8,000,000 bales were still warehoused—a carryover three times that of former years. For corn, the story was much the same, if more complicatedly told, since the bulk of the corn crop was fed to hogs on the farms where it was raised, then marketed as pork. Last year 71,425,000 hogs had been slaughtered, and the price per hundredweight had gone down from $6.16 the year before to $3.83. This year nearly 80,000,000 hogs were being prepared for market, and the market forecast was that if sold, they would bring farmers but $2.50 a hundredweight, a good deal less than the cost of production.

Kenneth S. Davis, *FDR: The New Deal Years, 1933–1937*. New York: Random House, 1986, p. 270.

Document 10: Roosevelt's Support of Suffering Artists

In this excerpt from her informative 1946 memoir about F.D.R., Frances Perkins, Roosevelt's secretary of labor, recalls his compassionate attitude toward poverty-stricken painters and other artists and his desire to include them in some of his relief programs. It is revealing that Roosevelt himself did not particularly care for most paintings (the principal exception being pictures of sailing ships); his decision to extend aid to artists stemmed mainly from his strong sense of humanity.

Roosevelt had a great many friends among artists. There was something natural and simple about most of them which made it easy for him to make quick contact with them. When the Civil Works project for work relief was getting under way, the decision to include artists in it was Roosevelt's own. A number of good, successful artists were greatly disturbed by the poverty and total loss of income which came with the depression to very competent painters. Alfred Barr, Director of the Museum of Modern Art, conceived the idea that artists should have the relief that other people were getting. He promoted it at every hand, mentioning it to a young girl who was a member of the family of a cabinet officer. Having no particular judgment about public affairs but being ardent about painting, she persuaded her reluctant parent to take it up with the President.

The President's immediate reaction was, "Why not? They are human beings. They have to live. I guess the only thing they can do is paint and surely there must be some public place where paintings are wanted."

He said paintings would look better than the old photographs and calendars which hung in public offices. So work was given to a great many artists at the standard of fifteen dollars a week that everyone else got. Post offices, town halls, schools, and other public buildings were covered with murals paid for at that wage and a great number of "easel pictures" were turned out in every section of the country. This, of course, led to other projects in the fine arts—music, theater, and historical research.

Roosevelt responded to the idea, not because he had any particular knowledge of the arts but because the people that practiced them were human beings and, like others, must earn a living.

George Biddle, the painter, once said of him, "You know, it is strange. Roosevelt has almost no taste or judgment about painting, and I don't think he gets much enjoyment out of it; yet he has done more for painters in this country than anybody ever did—not only by feeding them when they were down and out but by establishing the idea that paintings are a good thing to have around and that artists are important."

Frances Perkins, *The Roosevelt I Knew*. New York: Harper and Row, 1946, pp. 74–79.

Document 11: Roosevelt Explains the NIRA

In this excerpt from his July 24, 1933, fireside chat, the president describes, in simple terms, the main goal of the National Industrial Recovery Act (NIRA), submitted to Congress in May of that year.

Last autumn, on several occasions, I expressed my faith that we can make possible by democratic self-discipline in industry general increases in wages and shortening of hours sufficient to enable industry to pay its own workers enough to let those workers buy and use the things that their labor produces. This can be done only if we permit and encourage cooperative action in industry, because it is obvious that without united action a few selfish men in each competitive group will pay starvation wages and insist on long hours of work. Others in that group must either follow suit or close up shop. We have seen the result of action of that kind in the continuing descent into the economic hell of the past four years.

There is a clear way to reverse that process: If all employers in each competitive group agree to pay their workers the same wages—reasonable wages—and require the same hours—reasonable hours—then higher wages and shorter hours will hurt no employer. Moreover, such action is better for the employer than unemployment and low wages, because it makes more buyers for his product. That is the simple idea which is the very heart of the Industrial Recovery Act.

On the basis of this simple principle of everybody doing things together, we are starting out on this nationwide attack on unemployment. It will succeed if our people understand it—in the big industries, in the little shops, in the great cities, and in the small villages. There is nothing complicated about it and there is nothing particularly new in the principle. It goes back to the basic idea of society and of the nation itself that people acting in a group can accomplish things which no individual acting alone could even hope to bring about.

Quoted in William Dudley, ed., *The Great Depression: Opposing Viewpoints.* San Diego: Greenhaven Press, 1994, p. 117.

Document 12: Huey Long Calls for Sharing the Wealth

In 1935, Senator Huey P. Long of Louisiana presented to Congress his proposal for a national economic redistribution plan, asserting that the United States could overcome the ravages of the depression if it adopted the following measures.

Here is the whole sum and substance of the Share Our Wealth movement:

1. Every family to be furnished by the Government a homestead allowance, free of debt, of not less than one-third the average family wealth of the country, which means, at the lowest, that every family shall have the reasonable comforts of life up to a value of from $5,000 to $6,000. No person to have a fortune of more than 100 to 300 times the average family fortune, which means that the limit to fortunes is between $1,500,000 and $5,000,000, with annual capital levy taxes imposed on all above $1,000,000.

2. The yearly income of every family shall not be less than one-third of the average family income, which means that, according to the estimates of the statisticians of the United States Government and Wall Street, no family's annual income would be less than from $2,000 to $2,500. No yearly income shall be allowed to any person larger than from 100 to 300 times the size of the average family income, which means that no person would be allowed to

earn in any year more than from $600,000 to $1,800,000, all to be subject to present income-tax laws.

3. To limit or regulate the hours of work to such an extent as to prevent overproduction; the most modern and efficient machinery would be encouraged, so that as much would be produced as possible so as to satisfy all demands of the people, but to also allow the maximum time to the workers for recreation, convenience, education, and luxuries of life.

4. An old age pension to the persons over 60.

5. To balance agricultural production with what can be consumed according to the laws of God, which includes the preserving and storage of surplus commodities to be paid for and held by the Government for the emergencies when such are needed. Please bear in mind, however, that when the people of America have had money to buy things they needed, we have never had a surplus of any commodity. This plan of God does not call for destroying any of the things raised to eat or wear, nor does it countenance wholesale destruction of hogs, cattle, or milk.

6. To pay the veterans of our wars what we owe them and to care for their disabled.

7. Education and training for all children to be equal in opportunity in all schools, colleges, universities, and other institutions for training in the professions and vocations of life; to be regulated on the capacity of children to learn, and not upon the ability of parents to pay the costs. Training for life's work to be as much universal and thorough for all walks in life as has been the training in the arts of killing.

8. The raising of revenue and taxes for the support of this program to come from the reduction of swollen fortunes from the top, as well as for the support of public works to give employment whenever there may be any slackening necessary in private enterprise.

I now ask those who read this circular to help us at once in this work of giving life and happiness to our people—not a starvation dole upon which someone may live in misery from week to week. Before this miserable system of wreckage has destroyed the life germ of respect and culture in our American people let us save what was here, merely by having none too poor and none too rich. The theory of the Share Our Wealth Society is to have enough for all, but not to have one with so much that less than enough remains for the balance of the people.

Letter published in *Congressional Record*, 74th Congress, 2nd Session, vol. 79, no. 107, May 23, 1935: 8333–36.

Document 13: Father Coughlin Calls for Social Justice

Rev. Charles E. Coughlin, whose radio program drew between 30 and 45 million listeners in 1932 on the eve of Roosevelt's election and commencement of the New Deal, at first supported F.D.R. Later, however, Coughlin became one of the president's harshest critics and formed his own group—the National Union for Social Justice. Following is part of a 1935 lecture in which Coughlin sets the goals that he thinks will make America a prosperous and moral nation.

How shall we organize? To what principles of social justice shall we pledge ourselves? What action shall we take? These are practical questions which I ask myself as I recognize the fact that this NATIONAL UNION FOR SOCIAL JUSTICE must be established in every county and city and town in these United States of America.

It is for the youth of the nation. It is for the brains of the nation. It is for the farmers of the nation. It is for everyone in the nation.

Establishing my principles upon this preamble, namely, that we are creatures of a beneficent God, made to love and to serve Him in this world and to enjoy Him forever in the next; that all this world's wealth of field, of forest, of mine and of river has been bestowed upon us by a kind Father, therefore I believe that wealth, as we know it, originates from natural resources and from the labor which the children of God expend upon these resources. It is all ours except for the harsh, cruel and grasping ways of wicked men who first concentrated wealth into the hands of a few, then dominated states, and finally commenced to pit state against state in the frightful catastrophes of commercial warfare.

Following this preamble, these shall be the principles of social justice towards the realization of which we must strive:

1. I believe in liberty of conscience and liberty of education, not permitting the state to dictate either my worship to my God or my chosen avocation in life.

2. I believe that every citizen willing to work and capable of working shall receive a just, living, annual wage which will enable him both to maintain and educate his family according to the standards of American decency.

3. I believe in nationalizing those public resources which by their very nature are too important to be held in the control of private individuals.

4. I believe in private ownership of all other property.

5. I believe in upholding the right to private property but in controlling it for the public good.

6. I believe in the abolition of the privately owned Federal Reserve Banking system and in the establishment of a Government owned Central Bank.

7. I believe in rescuing from the hands of private owners the right to coin and regulate the value of money, which right must be restored to Congress where it belongs.

8. I believe that one of the chief duties of this Government owned Central Bank is to maintain the cost of living on an even keel and arrange for the repayment of dollar debts with equal value dollars.

9. I believe in the cost of production plus a fair profit for the farmer.

10. I believe not only in the right of the laboring man to organize in unions but also in the duty of the Government, which that laboring man supports, to protect these organizations against the vested interests of wealth and of intellect.

11. I believe in the recall of all non-productive bonds and therefore in the alleviation of taxation.

12. I believe in the abolition of tax-exempt bonds.

13. I believe in broadening the base of taxation according to the principles of ownership and the capacity to pay.

14. I believe in the simplification of government and the further lifting of crushing taxation from the slender revenues of the laboring class.

15. I believe that, in the event of a war for the defense of our nation and its liberties, there shall be a conscription of wealth as well as a conscription of men.

16. I believe in preferring the sanctity of human rights to the sanctity of property rights; for the chief concern of government shall be for the poor because, as it is witnessed, the rich have ample means of their own to care for themselves.

These are my beliefs. These are the fundamentals of the organization which I present to you under the name of the NATIONAL UNION FOR SOCIAL JUSTICE. It is your privilege to reject or to accept my beliefs; to follow me or to repudiate me.

Hitherto you have been merely an audience. Today, in accepting the challenge of your letters, I call upon everyone of you who is weary of drinking the bitter vinegar of sordid capitalism and upon everyone who is fearsome of being nailed to the cross of communism to join this Union which, if it is to succeed, must rise above the concept of an audience and become a living, vibrant, united, active organization, superior to politics and politicians in principle, and independent of them in power. . . .

This is the new call to arms—not to become cannon fodder for the greedy system of an outworn capitalism nor factory fodder for the slave whip of communism.

This is the new call to arms for the establishment of social justice!

God wills it! Do you?

Quoted in Daniel Aaron and Robert Bendiner, eds., *The Strenuous Decade: A Social and Intellectual Record of the 1930s*. Garden City, NY: Doubleday, 1970, pp. 159–61.

Document 14: Social Security Offers a "Measure of Protection"

At the historic signing ceremony of the 1935 Social Security Act, President Roosevelt thanked the Congress for helping give the American people a "patriotic" piece of legislation.

Today a hope of many years' standing is in large part fulfilled. The civilization of the past hundred years, with its startling industrial changes, has tended more and more to make life insecure. Young people have come to wonder what would be their lot when they came to old age. The man with a job has wondered how long the job would last.

This social security measure gives at least some protection to thirty millions of our citizens who will reap direct benefits through unemployment compensation, through old-age pensions and through increased services for the protection of children and the prevention of ill health.

We can never insure one hundred percent of the population against one hundred percent of the hazards and vicissitudes of life, but we have tried to frame a law which will give some measure of protection to the average citizen and to his family against the loss of a job and against poverty-ridden old age.

This law, too, represents a cornerstone in a structure which is being built but is by no means complete. It is a structure intended to lessen the force of possible future depressions. It will act as a protection to future Administrations against the necessity of going deeply into debt to furnish relief to the needy. The law will flatten out the peaks and valleys of deflation and of inflation. It is, in short, a law that will take care of human needs and at the same time provide for the United States an economic structure of vastly greater soundness.

I congratulate all of you ladies and gentlemen, all of you in the Congress, in the executive departments and all of you who come from private life, and I thank you for your splendid efforts in behalf of this sound, needed and patriotic legislation.

If the Senate and the House of Representatives in this long and arduous session had done nothing more than pass this Bill, the session would be regarded as historic for all time.

"Presidential Statement upon Signing the Social Security Act, August 14, 1935," Samuel I. Rosenman, ed., *The Public Papers and Addresses of Franklin D. Roosevelt.* New York: Russell and Russell, 1969, vol. 4, pp. 324–25.

Document 15: President Roosevelt Corrupted by Power?

In this excerpt from his book After Seven Years, *former Roosevelt advisor Raymond Moley, who became one of the New Deal's chief critics, accuses the president of succumbing to the age-old bane of rulers—the corruptive effects of holding and wielding great power.*

The one factor [of Franklin Roosevelt's character] of which I never dreamed was the intensifying and exhilarating effect of power upon such a temperament.

For Roosevelt in 1932 was not immodest. He listened patiently to advice. No one respected more than he the right of others to their own opinions. No one seemed less likely to be overwhelmed by the illusion of his own rectitude. He was the batter who had no expectation of making a hit every time he came up to bat. . . .

I would not have believed that Roosevelt would succumb to the unlovely habits of "telling, not asking," of brusquely brushing aside well-meant tenders of information and advice. . . .

I could not imagine that the quality of refusing to admit defeat would become the incapacity to admit error except in the vaguest of generalities.

I could not imagine Roosevelt's envisaging himself as the beneficiary of a vote based upon the challenge that he was the issue, that people must either be friends of the friendless, and hence "for him," or enemies of the friendless, and hence "against him."

I could not imagine that a growing identification of self with the will of the people would lead him on to an attempted impairment of those very institutions and methods which have made progressive evolution possible in this country.

But then, I did not reckon with what seemed, in a United States which cried out for action and assertion, perhaps the most irrelevant political axiom wise men through the ages had ever devised. I had not yet learned that no temperament, however fluid, is immune to the vitrifying effect of power. . . .

Power itself has ways of closing the windows of a President's mind to fresh, invigorating currents of opinion from the outside.

The most important of these ways is the subtle flattery with which the succession of those who see the President day after day treat him. Nine out of ten of those who see a President want something of him, and, because they do, they are likely to tell him something pleasant, something to cozen his good will. They are likely to agree with him, rather than disagree with him. If a man is told he is right by people day after day, he will, unless he has extraordinary defenses, ultimately believe he can never be wrong.

Until the very end of my association with Roosevelt, I hoped that his quality of pragmatism would keep some of the windows of his mind open. I finally found that he was not only being shut in by the usual process of flattery but that he himself was slamming shut windows. He developed a very special method of reassuring himself of his own preconceptions after hearing an unwelcome bit of advice. This consisted of telling Visitor B that he had just heard so-and-so from Visitor A and that A was "scared" about something, or that A didn't know what he was talking about. Usually B would agree with the President. But whether or not he did, if he was a man of spirit he decided that he, for one, wouldn't put himself into the position of being made ridiculous to Visitor C. So he would withhold all disagreement by way of self-protection. And so was another window closed.

Raymond Moley, *After Seven Years.* New York: Harper and Brothers, 1939, pp. 396–97.

Documents 16, 17, 18, and 19: Personal Memories of the Depression

Four people of very different walks of life here give their personal recollections of various aspects of the depression years. The first quote is a 1933 entry in the diary of Robert Carter, a young man who often lived the life of a hobo as he wandered across the country in search of work. In the second quote, Mary Owsley, who lived with her husband in Oklahoma from 1929 to 1936, remembers the terrible toll the crisis took on people in America's rural heartland. In the third, wealthy businessman Arthur A. Robertson, who did not suffer financially during the depression, describes other rich individuals who did. And the fourth quote is by George Tallen, in his teens and early twenties during the depression, who vividly recalls hard work, the repeal of Prohibition, and dealing with prejudice in the small Missouri town of Moberly.

Wilmington, N.C.

Stayed for two nights in the Y.M.C.A., sleeping on white beds in a warm room till I used up my welcome, then spent the third night in jail. It was pouring rain, the night cops were gathering and donning their slickers and rain hats. An old tramp was already there and later an intelligent, sharp-faced Jewish boy and a chance road companion came in. Their clothes were dripping wet and both were gray-faced with fatigue. After getting warmer, we gathered in an end of the building and began to talk so loudly and hysterically that the morose detective stared at us suspiciously. The Jewish boy said: "The old folks got theirs and we young fellows suffer. However, they've left us one great industry always open: there's always room for one more good hobo, so I take that. I'm going to California this winter to get warm."

In talking of our chances of getting anywhere in this world, the Jewish boy said our chances were damned slim. His pal, a smug, steady-eyed boy from Boston, grew a bit hot: "I can get along. Hell, a smart guy can always get along."

"Yeah? There's smarter men than you in the bread lines! What can you do? How you gonna get started?" I asked.

"Well, I won't be the only fellow that started with nothing in this world. I know I can find a good location somewhere and start a filling station." We gave him the horse laugh.

* * * * *

There was thousands of people out of work in Oklahoma City. They set up a soup line, and the food was clean and it was delicious. Many, many people, colored and white, I didn't see any difference, 'cause there was just as many white people out of work than were colored. Lost everything they had accumulated from their young days. And these are facts. I remember several families had to leave in covered wagons. To Californy, I guess.

See, the oil boom come in '29. People come from every direction in there. A coupla years later, they was livin' in everything from pup tents, houses built out of cardboard boxes and old pieces of metal that they'd pick up—anything that they could find to put somethin' together to put a wall around 'em to protect 'em from the public.

I knew one family there in Oklahoma City, a man and a woman and seven children lived in a hole in the ground. You'd be surprised how nice it was, how nice they kept it. They had chairs and tables and beds back in that hole. And they had the dirt all braced up there, just like a cave.

Oh, the dust storms, they were terrible. You could wash and hang clothes on a line, and if you happened to be away from the house and couldn't get those clothes in before that storm got there, you'd never wash that out. Oil was in that sand. It'd color them the most awful color you ever saw. It just ruined them. They was just never fit to use, actually. I had to use 'em, understand, but they wasn't very presentable. Before my husband was laid off, we lived in a good home. It wasn't a brick house, but it wouldn't have made any difference. These storms, when they would hit, you had to clean house from the attic to ground. Everything was covered in sand. Red sand, just full of oil.

The majority of people were hit and hit hard. They were mentally disturbed you're bound to know, 'cause they didn't know when the end of all this was comin'. There was a lot of suicides that I know of. From nothin' else but just they couldn't see any hope for a better tomorrow. I absolutely know some who did. Part of 'em were farmers and part of 'em were businessmen, even. They went flat broke and they committed suicide on the strength of it, nothing else.

*   *   *   *   *

In the early Thirties, I was known as a scavenger. I used to buy broken-down businesses that banks took over. That was one of my best eras of prosperity. The whole period was characterized by men who were legends. When you talked about $1 million you were talking about loose change. Three or four of these men would get together, run up a stock to ridiculous prices and unload it on the unsuspecting public. The minute you heard of a man like Durant or Jesse Livermore buying stock, everybody followed. They knew it was going to go up. The only problem was to get out before they dumped it.

Durant owned General Motors twice and lost it twice . . . was worth way in excess of a billion dollars on paper, by present standards, four or five billion. He started his own automobile company, and it went under. When the Crash came, he caved in, like the rest of 'em. The last I heard of him I was told he ended up running a bowling alley. It was all on paper. Everybody in those days expected the sun to shine forever.

October 29, 1929, yeah. A frenzy. I must have gotten calls from a dozen and a half friends who were desperate. In each case, there was no sense in loaning them the money that they would give the broker. Tomorrow they'd be worse off than yesterday. Suicides, left and right, made a terrific impression on me, of course. People I knew. It was heartbreaking. One day you saw the prices at a hundred, the next day at $20, at $15.

On Wall Street, the people walked around like zombies. It was like *Death Takes a Holiday*. It was very dark. You saw people who yesterday rode around in Cadillacs lucky now to have carfare.

One of my friends said to me, "If things keep on as they are, we'll all have to go begging." I asked, "Who from?"

* * * * *

Poverty is relative. We lived in poverty only we didn't know it. We lived much lower than most people on welfare today. But there were people who lived lower than us. We were sort of lower middle class. But we all worked. . . . I guess my early memories [of the Depression] are of working all the time. There was never a time in my youth when I could sit in a chair in [my] living quarters except when we had company. At noon, I'd walk home from school (about a mile), stay in the store (we had a small retail counter with candy and ice cream) while my dad and mother ate lunch, then they'd take over, I'd eat lunch and walk back to school. . . . The second biggest happening of that period (after the bank holiday) was the repeal of the 18th Amendment [Prohibition]. . . . This had a big influence on people, jobs, development, and community. Up until this time, the only place people could visit [in a small town] would be the confectionery. How long could you sit there with a sundae? [Most] people didn't sit in restaurants because they couldn't afford to eat out. When they did, it was in little places that were so small that there was no room to sit and visit. Now when we had our beer taverns [after Prohibition's repeal], people had a place to go. For a dime you could get a 32 oz. schooner of beer and could sit all day and night and talk and visit with everybody. . . . Nowadays [there is a misconception] that the only people who suffered prejudice [during the Depression] were black people. . . . That isn't true. . . . Poor whites [also] suffered prejudice. In the '30s [in] most places only the Irish had been accepted. The exceptions were where you had big populations of a certain nationality. Like in St. Louis, there were Greek neighborhoods, Italian, German, and various others. In the cities . . . they all lived together in their own neighborhoods. . . . But in most of the country (small towns and farms which had most of the population) there were not these large concentrations [of ethnic groups]. In Moberly, I was called a goddamned Greek—people would lean out of the car window to tell me to go back where I came from. The same for other national groups, mostly from eastern and southern Europe. . . . Jews—they had a bad time. My father told me to pay no attention. He said, "Do your work, do good at school, behave yourself, and laugh when people . . . try to berate you.". . . . Because I was able to get around the name-calling, I taught many other kids, mostly blacks, how to react [to prejudice] and [thereby] how to make their lives [a little] better.

Robert Carter quoted in Daniel Aaron and Robert Bendiner, eds., *The Strenuous Decade: A Social and Intellectual Record of the 1930s.* Garden City, NY: Doubleday, 1970, p. 48; Mary Owsley and Arthur Robertson quoted in Studs Terkel, *Hard Times: An Oral History of the Great Depression.* New York: Random House, 1970, pp. 45–46 and 66–67; George Tallen quoted from a 1997 interview with Don Nardo, first published in Don Nardo, ed., *Opposing Viewpoints Digests: The Great Depression.* San Diego: Lucent Books, 1998.

Documents 20 and 21: Roosevelt Attacks the Supreme Court

The following two documents relate to the 1937 controversy about the Supreme Court. The first is a March 9, 1937, AP news release describing how President Roosevelt claimed, in a fireside chat, that he wanted to reorganize the Court (mainly by increasing the number of justices) to make it more efficient and speed up its decision-making process. In reality, his aim was to stop the Court from declaring any more of his New Deal programs unconstitutional. The second news item, dated March 22, tells how a member of the Court struck back in a letter to the Senate Judiciary Committee. Ultimately, Roosevelt's Court reorganization bill failed to pass.

President Roosevelt called for swift enactment of his court reorganization bill tonight to "save the Constitution from the (Supreme) Court and the court from itself."

In outspoken fashion, the chief executive asserted the high tribunal had "improperly set itself up" as a "super legislature" and had read into the Constitution "words and implications which are not there and which were never intended to be there."

At the same time, he disavowed any intent to "pack" the court with "spineless puppets who would disregard the law" and decide cases as he might wish them decided, and asserted the processes of constitutional amendment were too slow for the pressing problems of the day.

His address, a "fireside chat" delivered from the small oval room on the ground floor of the White House, was the second devoted to a fighting appeal for passage of his bill to permit the enlargement of the court unless justices over 70 retire.

A major section of the address was devoted to answering the three most frequently heard criticisms of his proposal: that it is an effort to "pack" the court; that it would create a precedent which a future president, with dictatorial ambitions, could turn to his advantage; and that the solution of the problem lies rather in a constitutional amendment.

* * * * *

Chief Justice Hughes, in a letter presented to the Senate Judiciary Committee today by Sen. Burton K. Wheeler, Democrat of Montana, said that an increase in the number of Supreme Court justices "would not promote the efficiency of the Court."

The chief justice made it clear that he was commenting on an increase from the standpoint of efficiency and "apart from any question of policy," which, he said, "I do not discuss."

Mr. Wheeler, opening testimony in opposition to the Roosevelt court bill, began by reading the Hughes letter, which the chief justice said was approved by Justices Van Devanter and Brandeis.

The letter created a stir among the big crowd, which had assembled in the caucus room long before the hearing started, to listen to the Montana Democrat open the opposition to the court bill.

Justice Hughes was emphatic in his statement that the proposed increase in the number of justices "would not promote the efficiency of the court."

"It is believed," he added, "that it would impair that efficiency so long as the Court acts as a unit.

"There would be more judges to hear, more judges to confer, more judges to discuss, more judges to be convinced and to decide. The present number of justices is thought to be large enough so far as the prompt, adequate and efficient conduct of the work of the court is concerned.

"As I have said, I do not speak of any other considerations in view of the appropriate attitude of the court in relation to questions of policy.

"I understand that it has been suggested that with more Justices the court could hear cases in division. It is believed that such a plan would be impracticable. A large proportion of the cases we hear are important, and a decision by a part of the Court would be unsatisfactory."

Justice Hughes's letter was written to Mr. Wheeler in response to inquiries from the senator "with respect to the work of the Supreme Court."

The chief justice said that "on account of the shortness of time I have not been able to consult with the members of the court generally, but I am confident that it is in accord with the views of the justices."

"I should say, however," he added, "that I have been able to consult with Mr. Justice Van Devanter and Mr. Justice Brandeis, and I am at liberty to say that the statement is approved by them."

Justice Hughes began his letter with a statement that "the Supreme Court is fully abreast of its work."

Quoted in Associated Press Writers, *The Great Depression, 1929–1939*. Danbury, CT: Grolier, 1995, pp. 210–11.

Document 22: Roosevelt on the Impending World War

This December 31, 1940, letter by President Roosevelt was an answer to a recent communication from Assistant Secretary of State Francis B. Sayre. Sayre had expressed his worry that Japan might continue in its aggressive stance in the Far East, but he warned against the United States getting involved in a military conflict with the Japanese. Roosevelt's response, an appraisal of the international situation at the time, reveals his feelings about the chances of a world war. History has since shown that this appraisal was an accurate one.

Dear Frank:

The expression which you give me in your letter of November 13 of your pleasure over my re-election and of your good wishes for the critical four years that lie ahead is naturally most gratifying.

We of course do not want to be drawn into a war with Japan—we do not want to be drawn into any war anywhere. There is, however, very close connection between the hostilities which have been going on for three and a half years in the Far East and those which have been going on for sixteen months in eastern Europe and the Mediterranean. For practical purposes there is going on a world conflict, in which there are aligned on one side Japan, Germany and Italy, and on the other side China, Great Britain and the United States. This country is not involved in the hostilities, but there is no doubt where we stand as regards the issues. Today, Japan and Germany and Italy are allies. Whatever any one of them gains or "wins" is a gain for their side and, conversely, a loss for the other side. Great Britain is on the defensive not alone in and around the British Isles, and not alone in and around the Mediterranean, but wherever there is a British possession or a British ship—and that means all over the world.

You say that you have "the feeling that any day Japan may start moving southwards." As you point out, we are faced with the danger of Japan's continuing her expansion in the Far East, especially toward the south, while the European issue remains in the balance. If Japan, moving further southward, should gain possession of the region of the Netherlands East Indies and the Malay Peninsula, would not the chances of Germany's defeating Great Britain be increased and the chances of England's winning be decreased thereby? I share your view that our strategy should be to render every assistance possible to Great Britain without ourselves entering the war, but would we be rendering every assistance possible to Great Britain were we to give our attention wholly and exclusively to the problems of the immediate defense of the British Isles and of Britain's control of the Atlantic? The British Isles, the British in those Isles, have been able to exist and to defend themselves not only because they have prepared strong local defenses but also because as the heart and the nerve center of the British Empire they have been able to draw upon vast resources for their sustenance and to bring into operation against their enemies economic, military and naval pressures on a world-wide scale. They live by importing goods from all parts of the world and by utilizing large overseas financial resources. They are defended not only by measures of defense carried out locally but also by distant and widespread economic, military, and naval activities which both diminish the vital strength of their enemies and at the same time prevent those enemies from concentrating the full force of their armed power against the heart and the nerve center of the Empire.

The British need assistance along the lines of our generally established policies at many points, assistance which in the case of the Far East is certainly well within the realm of "possibility" so far as the capacity of the United States is concerned. Their defense strategy must in the nature of things be global. Our strategy of giving them assistance toward ensuring our own security must envisage both sending of supplies to England and helping to prevent a closing of channels of communication to and from various parts of the world, so that other important sources of supply and other theaters of action will not be denied to the British. We have no intention of being "sucked into" a war with Germany. Whether there will come to us war with either or both of those countries will depend far more upon what they do than upon what we deliberately refrain from doing. . . .

With best wishes for a good New Year, I am

Very sincerely yours,

[Franklin D. Roosevelt]

Quoted in Elliot Roosevelt, ed., *FDR: His Personal Letters, 1928–1945*. 2 vols. New York: Duell, Sloan, and Pearce, 1950, vol. 2, pp. 1093–95.

Chronology

1928

October—In New York during the national presidential campaign, Republican candidate Herbert Hoover delivers his "rugged individualism" speech, reemphasizing traditional American values such as self-reliance, and insisting that the federal government play a minimal role in people's lives.

November—Hoover is elected president, defeating his Democratic opponent, Alfred E. Smith, by a wide margin.

1929

October—The New York stock market crashes, sending the U.S. economy into a disastrous tailspin; in the following two years the nation sinks into a severe economic depression; the rest of the industrialized world quickly follows suit.

1930

December—The once-powerful Bank of the United States, along with many other smaller banks, fails; 4.5 million Americans are now unemployed.

1931

April—As the Great Depression tightens its grip, automobile tycoon Henry Ford lays off 75,000 workers.

1932

January—President Hoover signs into law the Reconstruction Finance Corporation, designed to help put banks and large businesses back on their feet.

July—Franklin D. Roosevelt, governor of New York State, gains the Democratic presidential nomination for the upcoming election.

September—Roosevelt delivers his "Commonwealth Club" speech, in which he asserts that government owes every citizen a right to life and a measure of security and happiness.

November—Roosevelt defeats Hoover in a landslide, winning the electoral vote by a margin of 472 to 59.

1933

March—U.S. unemployment reaches a devastating 15 million; Roosevelt is inaugurated as the thirty-second president; in his stirring inaugural address, he tells his countrymen that "the only thing we have to fear is fear itself"; the president shuts down U.S. banks and orders that their books be examined; Roosevelt gives his first radio "fireside chat"; the president submits to Congress the Agricultural Adjustment Act and the Civilian Conservation Corps, launching the massive legislative assault on the depression known thereafter as the New Deal.

May—Congress passes the Federal Emergency Relief Act, Emergency Farm Mortgage Act, Truth-in-Securities Act, and the Tennessee Valley Authority Act, the last of these designed to reshape the water system of the Tennessee River Valley and to provide cheap electricity for millions of Americans.

June—Congress passes Roosevelt's National Industrial Recovery Act and Home Owner's Loan Act.

December—The Eighteenth Amendment to the Constitution, prohibiting the sale of alcoholic beverages, is repealed.

1934

June—Roosevelt signs into law the Securities Exchange Act, which initiates federal regulation of trading practices.

July—The Federal Communications Commission is created, providing for federal regulation of radio, telegraph, and cable businesses; Congress passes the National Housing Act.

1935

April—Roosevelt creates the Resettlement Administration, designed to deal with the severe problems of rural poverty.

August—Congress passes the Wealth Tax Act, providing for higher taxes on well-to-do Americans; the president signs the Social Security Act, creating a national old-age pension system.

September—Louisiana's governor, Huey Long, who had proposed a widely popular wealth redistribution program ("Share the Wealth"), is assassinated in Baton Rouge.

1936

February—The Supreme Court declares the Agricultural Adjustment Act unconstitutional.

November—Roosevelt is reelected, defeating his Republican opponent, Kansas governor Alf Landon, by a crushing electoral margin of 523 to 8.

1937
April—The American economy finally reaches the level of output it had maintained in 1929 before the beginning of the depression.

May—The Supreme Court upholds the constitutionality of the Social Security Act.

August—With recovery seemingly taking hold, the nation experiences a sudden recession (economic downturn).

1938
June—Congress authorizes billions of dollars for new public works projects to fight the effects of the recent recession; Congress passes the Fair Labor Standards Act, providing for a minimum wage of 40 cents an hour and a forty-hour workweek.

1939
September—Raymond Moley, formerly one of Roosevelt's closest advisors, publishes his book, *After Seven Years*, in which he severely criticizes the president and the New Deal; war erupts in Europe as Germany, led by Nazi dictator Adolf Hitler, invades Poland.

1941–1945
The United States fights in World War II against Germany, Italy, and Japan; a virtual avalanche of American war production helps to pull the nation the rest of the way out of the depression.

1945
April—Franklin D. Roosevelt, architect of the New Deal and principal victor of World War II, dies at the age of sixty-three in the midst of his fourth term as president; he is succeeded by Harry S Truman.

For Further Research

Collections of Original Documents Pertaining to the Depression and New Deal

Daniel Aaron and Robert Bendiner, eds., *The Strenuous Decade: A Social and Intellectual Record of the 1930s.* Garden City, NY: Doubleday, 1970.

Associated Press Writers, *The Great Depression, 1929–1939.* Danbury, CT: Grolier, 1995.

William Dudley, ed., *The Great Depression: Opposing Viewpoints.* San Diego: Greenhaven Press, 1994.

Richard Hofstadter, ed., *Great Issues in American History: A Documentary Record.* vol. 2: *1864–1957.* New York: Vintage Books, 1960.

Harold L. Ickes, *The Secret Diary of Harold L. Ickes: The First Thousand Days, 1933–1936.* New York: Simon & Schuster, 1954.

William E. Leuchtenburg, ed., *The New Deal: A Documentary History.* New York: Harper and Row, 1968.

Robert S. McElvaine, ed., *Down and Out in the Great Depression: Letters from the "Forgotten Man."* Chapel Hill: University of North Carolina Press, 1983.

Diane Ravitch, ed., *The American Reader: Words That Moved a Nation.* New York: HarperCollins, 1990.

Elliot Roosevelt, ed., *FDR: His Personal Letters, 1928–1945.* 2 vols. New York: Duell, Sloan, and Pearce, 1950.

Samuel I. Rosenman, ed., *The Public Papers and Addresses of Franklin D. Roosevelt.* 13 vols. New York: Russell and Russell, 1969.

Studs Terkel, *Hard Times: An Oral History of the Great Depression.* New York: Random House, 1970.

Howard Zinn, ed., *New Deal Thought.* Indianapolis: Bobbs-Merrill, 1966.

General Studies of the Depression and New Deal

Anthony J. Badger, *The New Deal: The Depression Years, 1933–1940.* New York: Farrar, Straus, and Giroux, 1989.

John F. Bauman and Thomas H. Coode, *In the Eye of the Great Depression: New Deal Reporters and the Agony of the American People.* DeKalb: Northern Illinois University Press, 1988.

John Braeman et al., eds., *The New Deal: The National Level.* Columbus: Ohio State University Press, 1975.

Paul K. Conkin, *The New Deal.* Arlington Heights, IL: AHM Publishing, 1975.

Mario Einaudi, *The Roosevelt Revolution.* New York: Harcourt Brace, 1959.

Thomas H. Eliot, *Recollections of the New Deal: When the People Mattered.* Boston: Northeastern University Press, 1992.

Edward R. Ellis, *A Nation in Torment: The Great Depression, 1929–1939.* New York: Capricorn Books, 1970.

John K. Galbraith, *The Great Crash, 1929.* Boston: Houghton Mifflin, 1955.

James D. Horan, *The Desperate Years.* New York: Bonanza Books, 1962.

Edwin P. Hoyt, *The Tempering Years.* New York: Charles Scribner's Sons, 1963.

William K. Klingaman, *1929: The Year of the Great Crash.* New York: Harper and Row, 1989.

William E. Leuchtenburg, *Franklin D. Roosevelt and the New Deal, 1932–1940.* New York: Harper and Row, 1963.

Robert McElvaine, *The Great Depression: America 1929–1941.* New York: Tomes Books, 1984.

Milton Meltzer, *Brother, Can You Spare a Dime? The Great Depression, 1929–1933.* New York: New American Library, 1977.

Samuel Eliot Morison, *The Oxford History of the American People.* New York: Oxford University Press, 1965, pp. 935–87.

Michael E. Parrish, *Anxious Decades: America in Prosperity and Depression, 1920–1941.* New York: W.W. Norton, 1992.

Basil Rauch, *The History of the New Deal, 1933–1938.* New York: Octogon Books, 1975.

Arthur M. Schlesinger Jr., *The Coming of the New Deal.* Boston: Houghton Mifflin, 1959.

Bonnie F. Schwartz, *The Civil Works Administration, 1933–1934:*

The Business of Emergency Employment in the New Deal. Princeton, NJ: Princeton University Press, 1984.

Jordan A. Schwarz, *The New Dealers: Power Politics in the Age of Roosevelt.* New York: Knopf, 1993.

T.H. Watkins, *The Great Depression: America in the 1930s.* Boston: Little, Brown, 1993.

Social and Cultural Impact of the Depression and New Deal

Melvin Dubofsky and Stephen Burnwood, *Women and Minorities During the Great Depression.* New York: Garland, 1990.

James N. Gregory, *American Exodus: The Dust Bowl Migration and Okie Culture in California.* New York: Oxford University Press, 1989.

John B. Kirby, *Black Americans in the Roosevelt Era: Liberalism and Race.* Knoxville: University of Tennessee Press, 1980.

Walter Lippmann, *The Good Society.* Boston: Little, Brown, 1937.

Richard H. Pells, *Radical Visions and American Dreams: Culture and Social Thought in the Depression Years.* New York: Harper and Row, 1973.

Theodore Rosengarten, *All God's Dangers: The Life of Nate Shaw.* New York: Knopf, 1974.

John Steinbeck, *The Grapes of Wrath.* New York: Viking Press, 1939.

Susan Ware, *Beyond Suffrage: Women in the New Deal.* Cambridge, MA: Harvard University Press, 1981.

Herbert Hoover and the Hoover Administration

Herbert Hoover, *The Memoirs of Herbert Hoover: 1929–1941, the Great Depression.* New York: Macmillan, 1952.

William S. Myers and Walter H. Newton, *The Hoover Administration: A Documented Narrative.* New York: Charles Scribner's Sons, 1936.

Gene Smith, *The Shattered Dream: Herbert Hoover and the Great Depression.* New York: Morrow, 1970.

Harris G. Warren, *Herbert Hoover and the Great Depression.* New York: Oxford University Press, 1959.

Studies of Franklin D. Roosevelt and His Times

Kenneth S. Davis, *FDR: The New Deal Years, 1933–1937.* New York: Random House, 1986.

Frank Freidel, *Franklin D. Roosevelt: A Rendezvous with Destiny.* Boston: Little, Brown, 1990.

Joseph Gies, *Franklin D. Roosevelt: Portrait of a President.* Garden City, NY: Doubleday, 1971.

Gerald W. Johnson, *Franklin D. Roosevelt: Portrait of a Great Man.* New York: William Morrow, 1967.

Ted Morgan, *FDR: A Biography.* New York: Simon & Schuster, 1985.

Don Nardo, *Franklin D. Roosevelt: U.S. President.* New York: Chelsea House, 1996.

Frances Perkins, *The Roosevelt I Knew.* New York: Harper and Row, 1946.

Eleanor Roosevelt, *This I Remember.* New York: Harper and Brothers, 1949.

Legacy and Retrospectives of the Depression, Roosevelt, and New Deal

Wilbur J. Cohen, *The New Deal Fifty Years After: A Historical Assessment.* Austin, TX: Lyndon Baines Johnson Library, 1984.

Morton Keller, ed., *The New Deal: What Was It?* New York: Holt, Rinehart, and Winston, 1963.

Joseph P. Lash, *Dealers and Dreamers: A New Look at the New Deal.* New York: Doubleday, 1988.

Katie Louchheim, ed., *The Making of the New Deal: The Insiders Speak.* Cambridge, MA: Harvard University Press, 1983.

Raymond Moley, *After Seven Years.* New York: Harper and Brothers, 1939.

Edwin C. Rozwenc, ed., *The New Deal: Revolution or Evolution?* Boston: D.C. Heath, 1949.

Harvard Sitkoff, ed., *Fifty Years Later: The New Deal Evaluated.* Philadelphia: Temple University Press, 1985.

Index

Editor Biography

Historian and award-winning author Don Nardo has written and edited many books for young adults about American history and government, including *The War of 1812, The Mexican-American War, The U.S. Presidency, The Declaration of Independence, The Bill of Rights,* and *Franklin D. Roosevelt: U.S. President.* Mr. Nardo has also written several teleplays and screenplays, including work for Warner Brothers and ABC-Television. He lives with his wife Christine and dog Bud on Cape Cod, Massachusetts.